T0121343

CONNECTED

A Near-Death Experience and Its Aftereffects

P K BABCOCK

BALBOA.
PRESS

A DIVISION OF HAY HOUSE

Balboa Press books may be ordered through booksellers or by contacting:

Balboa Press
A Division of Hay House
1663 Liberty Drive
Bloomington, IN 47403
www.balboapress.com
1 (877) 407-4847

Because of the dynamic nature of the Internet, any web addresses or
links contained in this book may have changed since publication and
may no longer be valid. The views expressed in this work are solely those
of the author and do not necessarily reflect the views of the publisher,
and the publisher hereby disclaims any responsibility for them.

The author of this book does not dispense medical advice or prescribe the use
of any technique as a form of treatment for physical, emotional, or medical
problems without the advice of a physician, either directly or indirectly. The
intent of the author is only to offer information of a general nature to help
you in your quest for emotional and spiritual well-being. In the event you use
any of the information in this book for yourself, which is your constitutional
right, the author and the publisher assume no responsibility for your actions.

Any people depicted in stock imagery provided by Thinkstock are models,
and such images are being used for illustrative purposes only.
Certain stock imagery © Thinkstock.

Printed in the United States of America.

ISBN: 978-1-4525-9929-8 (sc)
ISBN: 978-1-4525-9930-4 (e)

Balboa Press rev. date: 12/17/2014

CONTENTS

Prologue - Connected

A NEAR DEATH EXPERIENCE (NDE)

YOU MUST GO BACK PETER. ITS NOT YOUR TIME AND YOU HAVE MANY IMPORTANT THINGS TO DO!

This is a story about a near death experience, that I was fortunate to have had and lived through. I will refer to it from time to time as an NDE for short. This wonderful NDE that I experienced, happened a long time ago, way back on September 21st, of 1960, to be exact

At the time, I was just twenty years old.

Back in those days, hardly anyone at all knew much about the phenomenon called a near death experience! In fact, I myself had never heard of it even being mentioned, let alone talked about, until it occured to me!

Today many of us have either known or heard of someone, maybe a friend, a relative, or quite possibly ones own self, who through a tragic accident or because of a critical illness, has experienced an NDE.

From time to time It also has been referred to, as an out of body experience, which of course it truly is!

These human souls have exited their body and have moved on from this world, to what most, if not all, believe to be a wonderland called Heaven.

It was definitely Heaven for me anyways, without any doubt whatsoever!

Those departed souls have then come back, all excited to tell the rest of us about this exciting journey they have just taken, along with the glorius place they have just seen!

The majority of these returned souls, including my own, did not want to go back into their earthly bodies, when their NDE was coming to its close!

Most IMPORTANT, this book is also about saving six people's lives.

For one reason or another those six saved souls were all in some kind of imminent peril!

I believe the six people, I helped to save, were all preordained for me to save, by my special Angel who accompanied me from Heaven, back to earth!

It's also about being in the right spot, at the right time to be able to help other people out in their time of needed assistance too!

To be sure, I had a lot of help from the Lord and/or the Angel in all of the life saving rescues, that I was Connected with!

I'm positive, they were also catalysts in the life helping situations too!

But what IF? What IF I had perished from the ruptured appendix, which, at the time, was a definite possibility?

Was there anyone else around to take my place? That answer I will leave up to you after you have read this book!

Speaking for me though, I would have to say a RESOUNDING NO!

WHY?

Because, It ALWAYS seemed like I was the only person in the general area that was able to HEAR or OBSERVE a bad situation that was already in the works, or a happening that was in the process of becoming one!

It also seemed like I was the ONLY ONE, that had the grit and/ or determination to get directly INVOLVED with whatever feat of courage was needed at the time to overcome the problem at hand!

There have been many books written on the subject of near death experiences, along with a great many television documentaries.

And now, even a full length movie, Heaven is For Real has been made frrom a recent book of the same name, about it!

Colton Burpo, the little boy in the Heaven is For Real NDE, suffered with the exact same, serious illness that befell me, namely a ruptured appendix with abscess. A very serious and unpleasent illness to go through for sure!

Just like Colton, I also am here to let everyone know, that most definitely, there is a special place called Heaven.

A Double Heavenly Colton/ Mr. Pete Connection!.....................

I know for certain, because my soul took an amazing trip there to visit this beautiful and wonderful place!

I'm going to prove it too! How, you ask? Very simple!

By witnessing my experiences in all of the IMPORTANT situations that happened to me in the months and years that followed my NDE. All these things occured just as the Angel STATED they would, in so many words! You might say some of those things were purely a coincidence. Yeah, maybe, but you can't go there alone, because there were just too many coincidences! Way to many!

As you get into the story you'll come to see just how much everything in my life seemed to CONNECT with everyone else and everything else.

They say that life is sometimes stranger than fiction. This book, as you will soon learn, is living proof of that statement!

I'm just going to give you the facts of all the wonderful things that happened and how everything played out, to the best of my recollection.

I'll leave it up to you to decide.

Remember, the proof is in the pudding, or so they say!

The book starts out with the Connections we all seem to have with each other plus other things, and how we are all affected by and also through these Connections!

Next will come WHY questions that we all seem to have from time to time, concerning all sorts of things with us. This is especially true of me with everything that went down following my severe illness! This will be followed by much of my formative years leading up to the Illness.

The severe Illness itself comes next!

My soul's escape from my body follows, with four Angels, helping to take me on a mystical journey to Heaven.

My soul eventually returns from Paridise with a single Angel by my side at the top of the ceiling in my hospital room.

This special Angel had a short but all powerful statement for me.

A STATEMENT that over time would prove to be so truly prophetic, time after time after time! And that strong message was:

YOU MUST GO BACK PETER, ITS NOT YOUR TIME AND YOU HAVE MANY IMPORTANT THINGS TO DO!

A pretty strong charge, from such a short statement, don't you think?

Following my return from Paradise, will come a jaw dropping office visit with Dr. James Kelly - Part 11, with his two astounding medical revelations, concerning me. Both of these amazing incidents, were also somehow Connected with him. Was I ever astonished when I walked out of his office that day!

Finally, starting with the blizzard at midnight will come much more detail of all the life saving rescues, along with the life altering help, I was able to provide and be involved with, through the months and years that followed my critical illness! Thanks to the Lord, along with the help of the Angel, all of this was possible because I survived the deplorable condition I was in!

According to medical science, when a person is in a coma, all brain waves cease to function. So it would be theoretically impossible to have any kind of a dream, let alone a near death experience while in this state of being! Theoretically, that is!

There was a book out recently, Proof of Heaven, by a noted Neurosurgeon, Dr. Eban Alexander, who at one time was himself a big skeptic on the subject of an NDE. He of all people experienced an NDE, and what was most unexplainable, while he himself was in a coma. Incredible to say the least! Needless to say, he is no longer a doubter on this blessed subject!

One person who (A future Dentist) I inadvertently assisted, happened TWO MONTHS BEFORE my near death experience even took place.

Looking back on this SPECIAL situation, I think this was a preparatory drill for me by the Angel of all the many important things to come! This one turned out to be One Heavenly Connection!.....................

Another person, who with the Lords help I was able to extract (My Friend Charlie) from a huge jam, happened three days before my 74th birthday on May 20 of this year, TWO FULL MONTHS after I started writing this book.

You can't make this stuff up!

All of the IMPORTANT THINGS that occured after my recovery, happened just as the Angels admonition to me, was stated, in so many (thoughts) words!

Always Remember, Just How Connected We All Are!...........................

WE'RE ALL CONNECTED
SOMEHOW

I chose to call this book CONNECTED, because in one way or another, thats what we all are! If you peel the onion back, far enough in time, aren't we all somehow related. The old saying, what goes round comes back round, would seem to fit, good, bad or otherwise! Or maybe life is just one big merry-go-round. We get on, we get off. People come and people go, but still we are all so intertwined with each other. What we choose to do or choose not to do, can and does send ripples through the lives of the rest of us, in one way or another.

Connections in out lives have a way of being everywhere!

At least in my lifetime, they have appeared far more often then not!

If you stop and think about it, probably in your lifetime too!

I would venture, way more than any of us ever realize!

Remember the old Christmas movie, It's a Wonderful Life starring Jimmy Stewart, who played George Bailey. George was a real good guy to one and all. He sacrificed everything he desired for himself, just to be able to help out his little New England town, along with all the people in it.

When Uncle Billy misplaced a large sum of money, George and the Bailey Savings and Loan, were in a big quandary. When things started going bad and everything seemed to be falling apart, George wished he had never been born!

His guardian Angel, who had just jumped into a roaring river to save his life, granted him his wish. Everything that once was good about this little town, was now bad and getting worse by the day. His wife was an old maid librarian and his children of course, had never been born, and all because George had never born!

Pandemonium was rampant and sadness was every where in the little town! All the people's lives that once were so Connected with George and what he did for them, were so much different now, and once again, all because George had never been born!

When George saw all the misery everyone was suffering, simply because he had never been born, he told his Angel he wished to be born again so everything could go back to being good, just like it was before.

An Angel/Reborn Connection...........................

What if I had perished back in 1960 from the ruptured appendix, which at the time was a genuine possibility. My four children and six grandchildren would never have been born.

Who would have been there to rescue those six people, all of which, were on the brink of disaster.

With the Lord's help, I was quite fortunate to somehow have been able to save those six souls from oblivion!

But if I had died, then what?

Who would have been there to help three complete strangers get food that they desperately needed?

Who would have even bothered?

Who would have been there to give Shorty a much needed respite at the station? Who would have even cared?

Who would have been there to give some transportation to a grandmother and her sick grandson? Once again, who would have bothered?

Who would have been there to change the ladies flat tire, the day I married?

Eventually, someone would have come along! Probably! Eventually!

As you'll soon learn, the six peoples lives, that for various reasons, were in imminent danger, were all somehow CONNECTED with my own!

One way or another, I knew them all! They were either neighbors or co-workers and one was a next door acquaintance! The first saved person was a teen age daughter of a railroad engineer, who I worked with and knew well.

By the way, not all people who are critically ill or tragically injured go through this wonderful phenomenon, which I experienced!

I guess you might say I was one of the lucky ones it happened to.

In my case, all things considered, I believe I was singled out for my grit, perseverance, and dogged determinationt to not ever give in or give up, no matter what!

As you'll discover in the following chapters, I was up to my eyeball's in either helping to save a life or drastically coming to the aid of a fellow human being, who needed some kind of earthly assistance at that MOMENT!

Pulling through my terrible illness, along with my NDE was the only piece of good luck I would have for the entire year of 1960.

In fact, it was the worst year of my life, before or since, in a multitude of a great many ways.

First and formost, in March my long time girl friend and I broke up and I never got over it, up to and including my illness, seven months later.

To make matters worse, the breakup was pretty much all my fault.

When I finally woke up and came to my sense's, that ship had already sailed!

At the time, she was the most precious person in the world, with a cute little dimple in the center of her chin! She was a little stubborn, but who in this life isn't. To be perfectly clear, I myself, could probably lead that parade! Later, when it came to the five life saving situations I would be confronted with, thank God I WAS STUBBORN and would not be deterred in the slightest, from the mission at hand! In those important situations, I would require all the stubborness I could possibly muster and then some!

Well, guess who was one of the X-ray Technician's at the hospital, when I became ill? if you said my old girl friend, you get an A+. I really didn't want her to see me in such a bad condition as this, but of course it couldn't be helped! I still loved her and didn't want her pitty.

Thats probably the main reason why I didn't go down to the hospital the day before to get throughly checked out. Stupid pride is never a good thing! The old saying; pride goes before the fall would certainly apply to me here!

One Sad Connection Here!......................................

In late August, my grandmother Ward and I had a fire in the apartment we shared, on Seneca St. We lost everything we owned except the clothes on our backs. If it couldn't get any worse, it just did. Our homeowner's insurance renewal policy, had somehow gotten misplaced and had now lapsed.

In just three short weeks away, I would be in the hospital, fighting for my life with a ruptured appendix, plus many other serious complications, including abscess and double pneumonia.

Doesn't sound too good, does it. Just wait, It gets WORSE! Much WORSE!

While in the hospital, a fellow employee and classmate of mine, Jerry Secondo came back from the Army and bumped me off my clerk's job with the Erie Railroad. He would later marry my operating room nurse technician, Margie pollinger. So now I was out of my job!

A Definite three way Connection here…....

I couldn't collect unemployment benefits from the railroad because you had to be employed as a railroad worker for a minimum of one year before that kicked in and I had only been employed there for seven months. Out of luck there. I also couldn't collect New York State unemployment from my previous job before the railroad because I needed a six month Connection there. Since I had a seven month Connection or one to many, I was out of luck there too!

Enough tough luck for one person, for one year, don't you think?

After my near death experience happened, I didn't quite know what to make of it, although It left me with one beautiful and lasting memory.

This NDE that I had, has stayed with me as vivid and fresh today as it was, when it happened, over fifty four years ago. Thanks be to God for our wonderful memories, at least the good ones!

When I first tried telling people about my NDE, they would either just pass it off, laugh in my face, blame it on the anesthesa, say I was dreaming. Also sometimes much worse, accuse me of making it all up.

Yeah right I thought, get a life!

It got to the point where I stopped talking about it altogether, as if it had never happened. But it did happen. It happened to me and theres no denying it. Not then, not now, not ever!

Everything that involved me, following my NDE, happened not for just any reason, but also for a Heavenly Connected Reason……..

Sometime in the late nineteen 1970s', when a lot more was known and was out there about this wonderful phenomenon, was when I once again started telling people, all about my own near death experience!

I would also tell them of all the many good and great things, I was involved with over the years that followed my near death experience!

Most people seemed to be all ears now and hung on my every word.

They would ask me all kinds of questions and I would answer them to the best of my recollection.

Laughing at me about my near death experience, was now passé.

It seemed as if everything had now come full circle.

So sad but true, it took many other people having a near death experience, for people, even some of my own family and friends, to believe that I really had gone through this wonderful experience!

My mom believed me right from the beginning, bless her heart so that's all that really mattered to me anyways!

She mentioned that around the time of my NDE she noticed a certain calm had suddenly come over me. A calm that she couldn't quite understand. She told me this happened sometime in the late afternoon after my operation.

She had just arrived at the hospital and said my eyes were half closed and that I had a large smile on my face!

Quite possibly this was at the moment my soul and body had become DISCONNECTED from each other!

Today only non-believers and doubting Thomas' it seems, have chosen to still cast doubt on this beautiful and glorious event!

All I would say to them, is too bad for you!

Finally an NDE Connection!............

WHY, WHY, WHY

As awe inspiring, as my near death experience was, there were going to be many IMPORTANT challenges that would ly directly ahead of me in the ensuing months and years that followed.

Particularly the thirteen years from February of 1961 through the summer of 1974.

I had no inkling of any of these IMPORTANT situations coming, but they were going to come, as surely as night follows day! In fact, just as my special Angel said they would.

I was ALWAYS going to be the FIRST RESPONDER, if not the ONLY one in all of these life or death situations!

Even to this day, I have a whole bunch of WHY questions, concerning all the difficult adventures that ended up coming my way!

WHY was I, the only person, to hear the frantic wails of a teenage girl in a farmers field of thigh deep snow at midnight, while at the same time, we both were being pummeled from all sides by a terrible blizzard!

Other men besides me, were coming and going from work in this immediate area, all at approximately the same time, and yet no one but me heard anything out there in that dark and foreboding field!

WHY? While no one else heard anything, I was able to hear her voice just as plain as if she was in the room right next to me! At first, I thought it was some kind of a joke or prank and that it was nigh unto impossible for anyone to be where I finally located her, on that incredible night so long ago!

Was I ever in for one big surprise!

When I finally came to the realization of the true predicament she was in, I took quick and aggressive action, going swiftly to her aid!

WHY did the Angel heap all of this responsibility on my small shoulders alone? Did he really have that much faith and confidence in me, when It always seemed that a whole lot of people, for who knows what didn't.

WHY did I fall asleep, late one night, on my sofa in my underwear, only to awaken to find a man passed out or maybe worse, on the steering wheel of his car? In a car, that was quickly filling up with thick black smoke, with no one else around! 99.9% of the time, I would have been fast asleep in my bed, at this late hour of the night. But on this ONE IMPORTANT night I wasn't!

WHY did I even bother to look out the kitchen window, when there was usually nothing to see at this late hour of the night?

Thank God something moved me to look out the window that night!

WHY did I just happen to come out of my home at the EXACT SAME TIME, two neighbor toddlers, two houses away, came tearing out of their home? They came down their steps on the fly, running for the road, fully unaware that at that very same time, a big garbage truck, was barreling down the road heading directly towards them! A perfect storm for a tragic accident was now in place!

WHY did I choose to DISOBEY and IGNORE the direct orders of my two superiors at the depot. Direct orders they gave me to not get involved in helping out a fellow emplyee who was now in a precarious situation!

This was a man who had fallen down and was now passed out, spread eagled, over a live and busy railroad track.

Without any hesitation whatsoever, I chose to go over their heads and head directly to his aid!

WHY did I happen to be home one night, in the right part of my duplex apartment, to be able to hear screeching brakes and screams, when an elderly neighbor was accidentally knocked down to the pavement and rolled under his car. No one else heard anything I guess, for as it turned out, I was the only responder, to those loud noises, on that hot summer night back in July of 1970.

WHY did I leave home way earlier then necessary, one cold, dark, December evening, to drive fifteen miles to take an important test, and in the process, picked up two hungry, hitch-hiking teenagers, and took them to a restaurant for something to eat.

HOW was it possible I ALMOST ACED this important test that I had failed so miserably twice before? It was a test I was very worried about taking for the third time! In fact I almost missed taking the test altogether, on account of helping out those two kids in their desperate time of need.

WHY was I accidentally, (or was it karma), passed over five times, for a seat in a restaurant. Everything that happened from that moment on, put me in the perfect position, to be THE PERSON, that was able to help out a lady and her sick, seventeen year old grandson. A grandson who was running a high fever and needed a ride to a hospital ER! Two waiters swore they never saw my name on the clipboard, but when I went back and looked, it was right there! Strange happenings to say the least!

WHY did I decide to pick up my check one hot, muggy Wednesday evening, when I ALWAYS picked it up on Thursday mornings.

Always, except this one night!

This SUBTLE CHANGE in my routine for ONE night, enabled me to be in the right spot at the right time once again. This time to lend a helping hand, to help out a fellow employee, in his desperate time of need!

Here was a man who looked horrible to me, with a gray pall over his entire face and who at the same time was experiencing chest pains, along with a definate shortness of breath!

WHY, two months BEFORE MY NDE ever happened, did I persevere so long and so hard to finally talk a friend into going somewhere he didn't want to go and just by his going, he would end up meeting his future wife on that very same evening! Just a coincidence, you might say. Yeah, right! I don't think so! Maybe more like one chance in five hundred million! Or more!

My persistince and dogged determination were in high cotton that night!

WHY was I once again in the right spot at the right time to catch a man taking some dress shoes from my friend John Todd's car. This poor soul was hungry and was going to try and sell the shoes to get some needed lunch money. In the process, I was able to not only save John's shoes, but MOST IMPORTANT, I was able to furnish the man with some much needed food! In the overall context of things, the delivered food was much more important then the delivered stolen shoes!

Make this One a Double Helpful Connection!.............................

WHY two months after staring this book, was I THE person that was able to find a scan gun misplaced at work, that had been lost for ten days. I found it on the eleventh day in less than three minute's after offering up a prayer to the Lord for his help in this tough situation!

I was drawn like a magnet, right to the spot where it had been misplaced, and in the process, saved my friend Charles his job!.........

The scanner was no match for the power of prayer on this day!

WHY was I in the right place and time to lend a hand, in helping out a candy salesman who was in a tough spot? Someone who I would never see again, but a stranger who would repay my help, with his generosity to me on that day.

LESS than a week later, his generosity paid to me, from a few days earlier would come back to greatly assist me in my own time of need!

This One ended up being a definite Reverse Connection!................

You can't make all or any of this stuff up!

Strange thing, but sometimes Karma has a hard time in finding us. Over my lifetime, it has found me again and again and again! Well, you get the picture!

WHY, WHY, WHY?

For me, the answer to all of these WHY questions would be one and the same!

DIVINE INTERVENTION - ALL OF THESE IMPORTANT THINGS WERE SURELY MEANT TO BE!......

Remember this! There are no mistakes with God.

Everything that happens, good or bad, happens for a purpose, or a reason, even if we mortals don't always agree with the end results....

At the end of my near death experience, as you'll learn, the angels parting words (thoughts) to me were:

"YOU MUST GO BACK PETER, ITS NOT YOUR TIME, AND YOU HAVE MANY IMPORTANT THINGS TO DO"!

One TEENY statement! One LARGE message!

Beyond any doubt in my mind, it was preordained for me to always be in the right place at the right time, along with taking whatever aggresive and decisive action that was needed at the time!

The Angel, as it turned out, would always be the message.

As for me, I was going to be his MESSENGER, fulfilling all of his prophecies, that he gave to me in that short but bold statement!

In one way or another, we were going to be CONNECTED with each other in this important and tender work!

Surely there were going to be some tough trials and tribulations ahead, but looking back in retrospect, everything turned out more then fine.

I would see a dangerous situation that had developed or was in the process of doing so, and I would go into swift action.

I never once hesitated, even for a moment, to think about any consequences, that might be Connected with the problem at hand!

When looking back, I'm sure my Angel was never too far away from me in any of those endeavors either! He had my back, of that I'm sure!

Remember, just as in sports, the best defense is a better offense.

There would be no time for any deliberation on my part in any of the five life saving events, that affected six prople!

Time would definitely be of the essence in all five of these affairs!

If I had known ahead of time, everything that ly ahead of me, I would have shuddered at the thought and really wondered whether I was up to the daunting task of facing them. As it turned out, thanks to my special Angel, along with much help from the Lord, I was way more than capable!

An Angel/human Connection!..........

Hang onto these two powerful and all consuming statements from Jesus! The first is; "You are to love the Lord and also love your neighbor with all your heart and all your soul." The second important admonition from Jesus is; "In so much as you did this for the least of me, you did it also for me!" All things depend on these two strong and important passages from the bible.

My belief is, we are all here on this earth for one main reason, and that reason being, to help each other out to the best of our ability.

Its called divine compassion and love for one another. It comes from God and resides in our soul!

Only God knows that we humans are all prone to err, make mistakes and sin!

Isn't that the reason they put erasers on pencils!

What other reason other then this, did Christ give up his life for us!

He didn't give it up because we're all-stars.

He gave his life up because we err, sin and need redemption!

I'm sure the Lord give's second chances, thirds too. Probably more!

Should we humans do any less?

He gave up his life to somehow save us from ourselves, if that's possible!

We all need to forgive each other from time to time, just as the Lord teaches us to forgive and move on from there. Don't be too hard on others and especially, don't be too hard on yourself either!

Always believe that things have a way of working themselves out.

And most of the time for the good, thank the Lord for that!

There's an old saying that goes like this; The wash always comes out. It may not always come out clean, but it always comes out!

From Humble Beginnings

I Was born Peter Karl Babcock in Hornell, N.Y on Thursday, May 23,1940, at 2:30am. I was born to Janet Kathleen Baker and Clifford Monroe Babcock.

Hornell is in the southwestern part of the state, an area often referred to from time to time as the Southern Tier, hard by the Canisteo River. The Canisteo can be a raging river, like it was during Hurricane Agnes, overflowing its banks, in late June of 1972.

Usually though, it is not much more then a shallow stream.

Whenever people ask me where I'm from and I tell them Hornell, their come back almost always is "I know where Cornell is, in Ithaca, N.Y." "No it's not Cornell, but Hornell." Then I have to go into much more detail, trying to explain where Hornell actually is. The original name of Hornell was Hornellsville named after a gentleman by the name of George Hornell.

Somewhere along the line in time, it was shortened to just Hornell.

Since I have always been extremely interested in the history of World War Two, I guess I picked an historical day, for freedoms sake anyways, to make my entrance onto the world stage.

At the time period surrounding my birth, Adolph Hitler and the German Army were running roughshod over all of Europe and he was in total control of most all of it. Most all of it that is, except for The British Isles.

Over 350,000 English soldiers and their allies, who were mostly Free French, were trapped at Dunkirk with their backs up against the North Sea.

It was a disaster ripe for the taking.

Hitler's Generals were eagerly awaiting his orders to either take these bedraggled troops prisoner or push them into the sea. Those orders, for some unknown reason never came and 99.5% of these troops were able to escape back to England by whatever means that was available; large transports, small boats, lifeboats, tug boats, sailboats and yes, even yachts.

Whatever was sea worthy at the time, was used for this desperate maneuver.

By the time Hitler finally woke up and gave the orders to move against this trapped army, most of them had now slipped through his fingers back to England, to fight yet another day. That other day of course would be June 6, 1944 or what would be better known around the world as D-DAY!

Hitler would forever regret his non-decision around May 23, 1940!

Heres' a real gem of a Connection of me with D-DAY.

While living in Canton, Michigan, in 1994, our home address was 6644 Whitehurst St. This important Connection never even dawned on me until one evening in early June. After coming back home from a three mile run,

I was bent over trying to catch my breath. I just happened to glance up at the address on the front of our house. It was as plain as egg on your face!

I'll be gosh darned if we don't have the D-DAY address, The 6th day of the 6th month of the year 1944, and now its almost fifty years later to the day. Five decades have now come and gone since that IMPORTANT day! I guess I was too busy with life, (which I was), to notice and Connect with it before, but there it was, in all its shining glory! WOW, what a remarkable Connection this turned out to be! Goose bumps broke out all over me!

No way to make this stuff up!

A Fifty Year Celebration Connection!…………..

I have the following lineage of being part; English, German, French, Irish, Italian and Dutch. You might say I was an original mutt!

As the old saying goes though, mutts make the most affectionate of pets!

Some of my English (Jeremiah Baker) ancestors helped to settle the land in and around the Hornell and Canisteo area, sometime in late 1778.

They, along with some other American settlers, had somehow escaped the Wyoming Valley Massacre!

This massacre was brought about by British troops from Fort Niagara along with the Tories (British sympathizers) and the Seneca Indians of the Iroquois Nation! They pillaged and burnt the fort near present day Forty Fort, Pa.

The most peculiar thing happened to me at work on Tuesday, September, 23, 2014. I met and waited on a customer by the name of Charles Baker from New Jersey. In our conversation, he told me he was into geneology of his fathers last (Baker) name. I told him about my moms maiden name(Baker) and the fact that my English relatives escaped the Wyoming Valley Massacre.

He related to me that he also had family that escaped the same Massacre, as me. WOW my thoughts!

Some bully Connection here!

His relation at the Massacre however were not named Baker but someone by the name of Hammond. His relatives finally ended up in the Elmira, N.Y. area while my relatives ended up 55 odd miles further west of them in the Hornell area. He wanted my phone number because he thought he might have some more information about my English (Jeremiah Baker) ancestor!

Later that evening, he called me with some exciting and unbelievable news! He located my Jeremiah Baker relative, who was many generations removed from a fellow by the name of Alexander Baker, from way back in early 1600. Charles said he was related to this Alexander guy and so was I.

So Charlie Baker, a customer from New Jersey and I were both relatives of these Baker men,from long ago. This made he and I some kind of relative to each other too! WOW, once again!

One Ubelievable Connection Here For Sure!........

Try and duplicate this one

I was not a planned child, but not many of us are anyways, in one way or the other.But always remember that we are all planned by God. At least our souls are! Whatever body he wishes to put them in is another matter. My mother and father however were not married at the time of my conception! I'm sure It was not a joyous moment for my father. He wasn't happy about it at all.At least according to my mom, her wasn't!

In the end, it didn't much matter to me anyways.

In addition to my loving mother, I had two wonderful and caring grandmothers plus two wonderful grandfathers, one of which was only a step-grandfather, but one who I absolutely loved.

I never had any kind of a Connection whatsoever with my paternal grandfather.

Although my mom and dad eventually married before I was born, it was not a marriage made in Heaven, no pun intended here. Not by a long shot.

It was always an on again, off again affair, mostly off.

My single mom and I moved so many times and so often, my head was in a perpetual spin, wondering where we might be headed for next.

I counted twenty three moves by the time I was twenty. Way too many!

It seemed we always had our suitcases packed.

We weren't poor but lower middle class would fit!

My mom's parents lived in Castile, N.Y., a small village of around 1,050 souls, about 37 miles west of Hornell, towards Buffalo. Mom and I would take the train to go and visit them until 1950 when the Erie Railroad discontinued passenger service between Hornell and Buffalo.

After 1950, we would go there by bus. This was no where near as much fun as a train, but it was the only public transportation available!

The passenger trains would make a comeback for a short while, sometime in 1961 after the Erie and the Lackawanna Railroads merged. That service would finally end for good in November of 1967.

There were a couple of times, when we lived in an apartment above Grandma and Grandpa Baker. There were also two other times during my young life, when I lived with them by myself.

Once was when my mom had a position with a bank in Buffalo. Another time was when she had another job with a bank in Warsaw, N.Y.

We also lived off and on many times with my paternal Grandmother Ward in Hornell. This was a perfect ingrediant for animosity between my mom and my fathers mother.

They would argue and bicker constantly, with grandma being mostly at fault, since she of course always took my fathers side and it definitely was the wrong side to take.

My father was never in the picture much during my early childhood and even less afterwards. He never saw me play little league baseball, high school basketball or even attended any of my track meets. Not once, not ever!

It never seemed to bother me or so I told myself anyways, but looking back on it, I'm sure it must have hurt. Probably a whole lot more than I ever let on that it did! So I had to fight that fight too, along with everything else!

This was especially hard on me, with all the other fathers, being there in attendance, most of the time!

With no reservation, I can say that I always tried to be there for my children while they were growing up, in whatever endeavor they were involved in.

When I was in the hospital in 1960 fighting for my life with the ruptured appendix, my father never came to see me once in the thirty days I was in the hospital, and he lived just FIVE minutes away. My mom was at the hospital every day though, so that's what really mattered to me anyways!

My step mother came to see me three or four times too. My old girlfriends mom came to visit me a few times, which I really appreciated, since I loved her too!

I remember one time in early June of 1944, right around D-DAY ITSELF, when I had just turned four. My grandparents lived on Beechwood Avenue at the time. Beechwood Ave. wasn't an avenue at all, just a small street in Castile, with eight or nine houses on it. At the top end of the street there was a huge dark forest. Being only four years old, it sure looked huge and dark to me anyways!

On this day, Grandpa Baker took me into the forest with him to pick blackberries. He had picked a half of a pail of berries and sat me down on a fallen log, while he went into a much deeper thicket where he had spied some bigger ones. When he returned, I had eaten a great deal of the berries he had entrusted to my care and I had berry juice all over my face.

I knew I was in big trouble when he called me Peter. "Peter, we're in for a lot of trouble with your grandmother."

"She was planning on those berries for a blackberry pie tonight."

He must have had enough berries or he picked some more, because we had blackberry pie for dinner that evening. Grandma never knew of my berry thievery. Of course grandpa and I never told her. Ah for the love and secrecy of grandfathers! The old addage; "What they don't know won't hurt them" was in play here!

The big news from the radio that night was D-Day the sixth of June had finally arrived in Europe. America and her Allies had a firm foothold in Normandy, after a horrendus first day of fighting!

Hitler's goose was finally about to be cooked!

After dinner on Christmas Eve in that same year of 1944, Grandpa Baker asked if I would like to go and see a minature toy train on display in the village hardware store window. "Can we," was my quick reply.

We walked the two short blocks to the hardware store in a heavy snow storm, something like what our soldiers in Europe, were now experiencing while fighting the Battle of the Bulge in the Ardennes. Same Christmas Eve, but two separate worlds far apart!

Grandpa and I watched in the pitch darkness, with snow falling all around us, as an american flyer Engine and ten cars with a red caboose kept circling around a big and beautifully lit Christmas tree. I was so little grandpa had to pick me up just to see the train through the window.

Talk about being in Heaven if only a few years early.

I didn't know it at the time, (how could I at four) but in just sixteen short years away, I would be working around real trains, at the same time while working with real railroad men too. Unreal that they would pay me for doing this job. And pay me well too, along with great benefits!

What a lifetime love affair that would turn out to be.

Some of my best childhood friend's lived in Castile.

Harlan and Rebecca Allen, my best bud's lived three doors away from my grandparents. Bobby Davis lived next door. Bobby's family was one of the first to have a TV in Castile and he would always invited me over to his house in 1949 and 1950 to watch Howdy Doody, which came on the air from 4:00 to 5:00pm Monday through Friday. It was broadcast from a TV station in Rochester, N.Y.

I think the call letters of the station were WROC. He received one other channel, WBEN out of Buffalo,N.Y. There was no cable, just rabbit ears!

Before four oclock and after five, there was only a test pattern on the TV. Everything was in black and white too. Quite a big difference from the twenty four hour, cable, color televised programs of today.

The Davis' would travel to Warsaw, Perry and Fillmore, N.Y. on Friday or Saturday nights to the movies and would invite me to go with them, which I was more then happy to oblige.

Since none of my male friends liked sports, Rebecca and I would play baseball or football catch with each other.

She was pretty gosh darn good at it too.

In the winter we didn't even get dressed for school until we first listened to the school snow closings. Lake Erie effect snow storms, dumped tons of the white stuff on the Castile area. Somewhere around 100 or more inches per winter, would be a good guess. The snow would start sometime in November and last until the end of March, sometimes even into April.

Grandpa was the manager of the Dewitt and Boag Silk Mill in Castile. He had 40 to 50 employees, mostly women, who worked for him in the mill.

He would get up sometime around 4:30am, go down to the mill, which was one short block away and line up the raw material for the day's work.

In Winter he would fire up the coal based furnace so it would be warm and cozy by the time the women came into work.

The looms made so much noise banging back and forth, you couldn't carry on a normal conversation. Even if you screamed in the other person's ear.

To carry on any kind of talk, you would have to go outside the mill.

Working day after day in this loud environment, must have been terrible on those ladies hearing.

The ladies would report for work at 8:00am. Sometime after 8:30, grandpa would come home, eat breakfast and lie back down until lunch time. After lunch he would go back down to the mill until sometime after 5:00pm when he would close the plant up for the night. He did this every week for years and never wavered, until he was felled by a detached retina.

When lifting a heavy bolt of silk sometime in the summer of 1950, he suffered a detached retina in his left eye. While undergoing surgery to reattach the retina at a hospital in Buffalo, he sustained a minor heart attack, along with blood clots. He would never work again after this serious setback. Without his managerial leadership, and with no one else qualified to replace him, the mill folded up a few months later.

I'm sure I got my work ethic from him!

During the last twenty-five years of my thirty-seven year railroad career, I worked an average of right around sixty hours a week. Every week except vacations that is! A couple of years, I even worked a few vacation days!

It was all mental and somtimes it could be quite strenuous.

I had the business of the railroad to take care of first and formost, but at the same time I always tried to look out for the men too, to the best of my ability!

Some of the men never realized it and some never appreciated it, but MOST of them did, thank God!

One July evening in 1996, while working for Conrail in Dearborn, Michigan, co-manager Trig Haug and I had worked nine straight ten to twelve hour days. At the time, we had two managers on vacation and another one was off sick.

When we reported for work at midnight on our tenth straight day, our big boss Wayne Richards from Philadelphia went up one side of us and down the other. He was a super boss, but on this day he wasn't happy with us at all!

He had us on a three way speaker conference call and he was livid.

"What are you two guys doing there?" "Didn't I tell you both last night not to come into work tonight?"

We tried to argue our case to him. Trigger started the conversation and I backed him up. "We need to be here Wayne, because we have over thirty trains standing all over the railroad for the want of an engineer, conductor, or both and we need to help the crew dispatchers find crews for them."

I added; "No way we can do it from home and Its costing us a ton of money for these trains to just sit idle."

Now he gave it to us straight. "I don't much care if the railroad stops running altogether." "I'm much more worried right now about the two of your guys health and I want the both of you the heck out of there and gone home right now, do you both understand me?" "Yes sir we do." "How about you Pete?" "Yes sir Wayne, I do!"

"Take a couple of days off, God knows you both deserve it and then the both of you can come back and fight this battle another day, ok?"

"And oh, by the way, I also want to thank the both of you for your continuing dedication."

The both of us ended up taking just the one night off, rejoining the fray the next night. Funny thing happened Connected with this. Neither of us knew the other one was coming in the next night, since we were both told to take two days off. However both of us didn't want to leave each other in the lurch just in case he came in. For that reason we both came in! When we saw each other, a huge smile broke out on both of our faces! We had each other's back on this one, big time!

We were surely deadicated to the railroad, but dedicated to each other too!

Once again. you can't make this stuff up!

Two Connected Railroad Managers!.............................

Grandpa Baker passed away from a blood clot and conjestive heart faiure on March 10 of 1956 at the age of 68. I wish I had seen him along with Grandpa Ward on my NDE to Heaven back in 1960, but I'm positive I will on my next and final trip there. That is, if I'm deemed worthy enough to get a second trip. That of course will have to be determined when the time comes by someone way much bigger then me!

Grandpa Ward was a keeper too. He was one kind and sweet person, especially to me. Although we were not blood relation, there was a strong CONNECTION between the two of us. We loved each other dearly.

Once in 1949, just before the trains to Buffalo stopped running, he left Hornell on the morning westbound train, met me at the station in Castile and took me to Warsaw, N.Y. for an afternoon movie. Afterwards we had dinner together at a restaurant. Then we reversed the move on the evening eastbound train, droping me off at Castile and then grandpa going on alone to Hornell. He just wanted to spend some time with me, bless his heart.

I'm so sorry that I was too young too fully appreciate the moment.

Grandpa Ward died of a heart attack in the Spring of 1953 at the young age of 63. Certainly way too young by todays standards.

I lost the two most important men in my life at the young and tender ages of twelve and fifteen. By the way, Grandpa Ward did get to see some of my Little League games. I pretended he wasn't there, but believe me, I knew!

My old girlfriends mother who I loved dearly and Grandpa Ward both rest in the same cemetery in Hornell, separated by only thirty feet of grass. However, both of these gentle souls, now call Heaven home!

Two Good and Caring souls Forever Connected With Me!.......

Grandma Baker was of pure German stock, through and through!

Her parents were both born in Germany sometime in the early 1860's and migrated to America sometime in the 1880s.

24

Grandma was born in 1893 and was way ahead of her time in many, many ways. She made me take vitamins and cod liver oil every day. Ugh!

I had to wash my hands after every trip to the bathroom, which was quite understandable. Before eating was also a must, along with as many other times during the day as she deemed necessary, which were way to many times for me.

In addition to all of this, I had to chew every mouthful of food twenty five times before swallowing. Try doing it sometime. Not an easy thing to do!

At least not over and over and over!

This of course was to aid in digestion, which she was right about once again, since 75% of our digestion is done in our mouth before we ever swallow any of our food.

I could use very little salt too. She always mentioned the fact, that we had to protect our kidneys along with our blood pressure. Right once again!

Remember too, we're talking about the mid to late 1940s here!

There was no talking at the dinner table while eating and everything was steam cooked in a pressure cooker. She made the best Christmas cookies and her homemade strawberry shortcake was my favorite dessert of all time.

Add blackberry and cherry pies also, to that list.

In fact Blackberry pie was my all time favorite pie, I wonder why?

Dinner was at 6:00pm sharp, while we listened intently to the radio vibes of John Cameron Swaze, Morgan Baby and Walter Winchell, while taking the full hour between 6 and 7:00pm to eat. There was no 7:00pm evening news on the TV, like there is today. That was still a few years away.

Walter Winchell's entrance line was always; "Good evening Mr. and Mrs. America and all the ships at sea." For some reason that has stuck with me for all these many decades.

Since we didn't talk much, the only sound beside the radio, was the ticking of a Baby Ben clock on a bureau right behind me.

Both evening trains arrived at the station sometime between 6:00 and 7:00pm. They might even show up together if one train was running late. You could hear their sad and mournful whistle's as they blew for the crossings coming into or leaving town.

I got so I could tell each train from the other just by the sound of their whistle and the location of their train. Kinda neat, I thought.

Grandpa would always ask me whether it was an easbound or a westbound.

Grandma had a slight limp caused by a car accident when she was in her late twenties, but it never seemed to slow her down much, at least not any that I could ever notice anyways.

If she told you to march, you had better be prepared and have the rifle already on your shoulder. You had better be ready to halt too, maybe even before the order was given.

In all fairness to her though, she always had my best interest at heart, even if I didn't think so at the time. She took me to church every Sunday when I lived with them, which was a good thing, learning all about Jesus.

I was always in the Christmas play at church, usually one of the wise men.

I always wanted to play the part of Joseph since he was Jesus's father on earth and to me he was a very important figure, which he surly was!

The trash and garbage were picked up by a couple of brothers, Rube and Josh Billings, who lived with their mother in a nice house, not far from Grandma's. They used a team of horses and an old wagon for their job.

I loved the horses and from time to time they would let me pet them.

One of the horses was named Daisy, but I don't remember the other.

They always told me they were going to get me a pony and I believed them, but of course it never happened. They had a fish(me) on the line and they weren't about to let it off the hook, anytime soon. Not if they could help it.

One hot day in the summer of 1949 behind Bobby Davis's house, we were all jumping off a large pile of boards into high grass.

On my third jump, I landed squarely on a hornets nest. I came running and screaming to the back of my grandmothers house, with the bees in hot pursuit. My mother quickly came out and drove the bees away with my grandfathers garden hose.

I must have been stung twenty five to thirty times all over my head and body. Mom and the next door neighbor, Mrs. Hubbard made mud patties and applied them to all the bee stings, which helped me immensely.

By dinner time the bee stings were a lot better, but what a terrible experience that one turned out to be!

In the summer time a school bus would pick us up three times a week and take us to Silver Lake, five miles away to go swimming.

The water temperature was right around sixty five degrees, but we jumped right in anyways. I enjoyed the ride on the bus as much or more than jumping into that frigid lake.

Castile was a fun place to be, especially in the summer, but I missed Hornell and always looked forward to going back there.

Since I lived there the most, It seemed more like home to me.

One big fact was Grandma Ward was not as much a disaplinarian as Grandma Baker was and she was a whole lot easier on me.

Being a kid, I guess I liked that.

Grandma Ward would fix me what I wanted to eat instead of having a set menu and of course I liked that better too.

She didn't like it, but she did let me drink Pepsi Cola.

Hornell meant going to the municipal swimming pool, where the water was a whole lot warmer than Silver Lake. The cost was a quarter plus a dime for a locker. A bargain at any cost.

There were four movie theatres; The Strand, Hornell, Steuben and Majestic.There were two double feature westerns every Saturday, starring either Gene Autry, Roy Rogers, Hopalong Cassidy, and John Wayne.

Also my favorites, Wild Bill Elliott as Red Ryder with Robert Blake as Little Beaver.

The Strand closed in the early fifties, but the other three theatres kept pace with each other for at least twenty more years. The end came for two of the three left with the popularity of television the population being decimated by the railroad leaving town!

There was a Class D minor league team, the Hornell Dodgers, which was a farm club of the Brooklyn Dodgers right up to and including 1957.

There was Little League Baseball for boys eight through twelve and Junior League for boys thirteen through eighteen. There were four baseball fields to play on and four tennis courts, all at Maple City Park.

Elmhurst Dairy made the best milkshakes I've ever had for just twenty five cents. It cost ten cents for extra malt, if you wanted some.

They also produced the best cottage cheese, I have ever tasted too.

We had two nice state parks close by. Letchworth and Stony Brook, both less than an hours drive away. Both parks had swimming pools and beautiful views from nice walking paths. Stony Brook's pool was spring fed and it was super cold even if the air temperature was in the nineties. When you dove in the water there, it woke you up in a hurry!

The two pools at Letchworth were a whole lot warmer.

I loved going to those places. The only drawback was, we had no car, so that made it hard for us to get there very often.

We had socials (dances) for older teenagers almost every Friday night at the high school and Saturday night at the Foxhole of the YMCA, a youth hangout. Twenty-five cents was the price of admission to these dances. There was a roller skating rink, a Taste Freeze that made soft ice cream and a drive-in theatre. You name it, we had it.

If there was one thing in Hornell, that I missed, it was the lack of public basketball courts to play on or just to shoot baskets on!

When they would let me, I would play on the private courts of some of my friends, Ned McHenry, Mike Spitulnik or Jimmy and Larry Gleason.

Lowell "Curly" Walkers father had a beautiful half court built for him behind their home in North Hornell. It was a state of the art court and everyone wanted to play on it. You usually had to take a number just to play.

They had a detached garage which was always open with three or four basketballs lying around to use. What a good deal that was too.

Although it was more than a mile from my place, I was there quite often because of my love of the game coupled with my desire to always get better.

Remember the old adage; Practice makes perfect. I guess I adhered to that statement 100%, maybe even 125%!

I went from not being able to play at all to being pretty gosh darn good!

Especially when my size was taken into consideration.

It took me literally many years of practice, along with much determination to bring forth the talent the Lord had blessed me with.

Sometimes before Curlys court was built, we would go in someone's car to Canisteo, five miles south of Hornell to play. They had a real nice outdoor full court. They also had a fine group of players; David Jack, Pete Etu, Larry Taylor, John Lee Jamison and Pat House to name a few.They never seemed to mind us coming down to play with them or against them and they looked at us as good competition, which of course we were.

Much more about basketball in the next chapter.

In later years I would referee high school games with both John Lee and Pat.

In the early 1950s if I couldn't find anything else to do, I would jump on a city bus, and for a dime, ride all around town on the bus route, and talk to the bus drivers. Sometimes for an hour or more.

I knew them all on a first name basis. My favorite was Louie. He had false teeth, but wouldn't wear them. He would talk your head off. I loved riding with him! All of those bus drivers are long gone now! The near end of the bus route was at the Car Barns on Adsit St, where the old trolly cars and the bus's after them, would park for the night. The far end of the route ended at East Avenue, right before the railroad tracks, next to the huge railroad yards.

Little did I realize it then, but in a little less then eleven years, a teenage girl and I would be having a rendezvous in this general area.

It would be in the middle of a farmers snowy field at midnight, with a terrible blizzard raging all around us. It would be one surreal and tenuous situation. Sometimes, its a good thing we don't know what lys ahead of us! For me, this was truly one of those times!......

One hot Summer day when I was nine or ten years old, Dale Hendee, a childhood friend of mine, suggested we ride our little bikes to Stony Brook State Park for the day. Not a very good idea, but it sounded good to me!

To compound matters for us, we decided not to tell our mothers we were going for fear they wouldn't let us go. Boy, was that ever a positive thought.

Besides, we would be back long before they even knew we were gone, or so we thought anyways! Wrong on that count too. It was about a thirteen mile one way trip to the park! What were we thinking? I guess we wern't!

Once at the park entrance it was still almost another full mile to the natural stone formed, spring fed pool.

We left Hornell at 8:30am, arriving sometime at the park around 2:30pm.

After swimming and resting for a short while, we figured it was time to head back home. To be sure, we didn't look forward to the return trip

Leaving the park, we had to walk our bikes up a mile long steep hill.

Upon reaching the crest of the hill, we were totally and completely drained. We hardly had any strength left to pedal the bikes home.

As it turned out, It was way more of a trek than we had anticipated.

Dale was about ready to give up, but I kept prodding him to keep going, that we would make it, and that we just had to keep going!

By the time we hit Hornell, sometime around 8:45pm it was getting dark.

We needed water real bad and were famished for food.

Sheer grit and determination saw us through this day!

By this time, our moms had the city police out looking for us.

My mom was so glad to see me, she couldn't stop crying and hugging me.

I was amazed that there was no spanking, not even a lecture.

The next day was far different. I got the spanking of my life, with my mom's hair brush.Ouch!

She said she couldn't do it the night before because she was just so glad to see me and knowing that I was alright. The more she thought about it though, the madder she got!

At least that was her story and she was sticking to it.

Needless to say, it was the last time I did anything like that on my own.

Another time, Sarah (Sally) Harris, a classmate of mine in the fifth grade at the Columbian Elementary School and I went to the movies together one Sunday to see Tea For Two, starring Doris Day and Gordon McCrea. Sally wanted to stay and see the movie over again so we did, and got in hot water with our mothers even though they knew where we were.

They found us sitting in the back of the Steuben Theatre, munching on some popcorn. No spanking this time. I guess no harm, no foul!

Someone once asked me what was the best decade I have lived in.

Without any hesitation, my answer was the 1950s followed close by the 1940s. No other decade even comes close.

It was a time when you could leave your car keys right in the ignition, even overnight. You could leave your front door unlocked, even after dark. People would just knock and walk right in, announcing as they came. Everyone knew everyone else on a first name basis and everyone was a good neighbor to one and all.

This was truly the last age of innocence.

People genuinely cared about each other and pitched in wherever and whenever they could. Not for any monetary amount they would gain, but just for doing what was right.

I recall my girlfiend had an elderly, next door neighbor lady whose toilet kept running. Alhough not mechanically inclined, I fixed it for her without her even asking for help, but just for the fact of her mentioning that the chain had slipped off the flusher in the tank and she couldn't fix it.

Jean and I were married on Saturday, September 22, 1962 at a Methodist Church in Greenwood, N.Y.

On the way to pick up her sister Arlene and brother-in-law Don, who were going to stand up for us, we passed a car stopped on the shoulder of the road with its trunk lid propped open.

Two ladies were standing in the shade nearby with worried looks on their face. I pulled over to the shoulder of the road just ahead of them and walked back to check on their problem. They had run over something in the road and had sustained a flat tire on the passengers side rear tire.

They had a good spare tire and tools alright, but little if any knowledge whatsoever of how to change the tire.

I told them not to worry, I would be right back.

I went back to my car and took off my sport coat, tie and short sleeve white shirt, just leaving me in a t-shirt.

"What are you doing back there anyways?"

"These two ladies have a flat tire and don't know the least how to change it, so I'm going to help them out and change it for them."

"You do know, don't you that we're getting married today."

"I know and we will, but first I've got to take care of this problem."

Since I had never changed a tire by myself, I was flying by the seat of my pants on this one. Much to my surprise, I got her done!

It took me about forty-five minutes to complete the task and happily, the ladies were on their way, once again.

Just one more Connection, I guess I had to make!................

We had four children; Michael, Susan, Scott and Beth. We were married a little more than thirty-six years. We had a lot of good times and a few bad ones, but once the kids were grown, we had hardly anything in common and the marriage ended amicably.

LITTLE LEAGUE
AND BASKETBALL

Little League baseball came to Hornell in the Spring of 1948.

In fact I thought it was named after me, since I was so little. I was in love with baseball instantaneously. I had the drive and desire alright, but not quite the size or ability and therefore I was cut after my first three day tryout with one of the teams. Not too many boys who got cut from athletic teams back in those days were willing to try again.

Maybe the failure of being cut hurt so bad, (and it did) that once was more than enough pain and humiliation to suffer. In my case, it just seemed to make me more resolute and determined than ever. I didn't care what humiliation or pain I was going to suffer, I was eventually going to make it, and that's all there was going be to it! End of story!

I had a driving spirit deep inside me to overcome and succeed and that fire never went out! I got cut as a nine year old, and again as a ten year old.

While still not very big, I finally made it as an eleven year old, and as a twelve year old I batted .430 and was an alternate second baseman for the All Star Team.

Funny thing, but I couldn't even start at second base for my own team, the K OF C (Knights of Columbus). How could that be possible you ask?

Well, our managers son had to play there. Nepotism was at play here!

This was my first real taste of discrimination of any kind and it didn't sit to well with me. Sadly, it would be far from the last!

Our game times were either at 5:00pm or 6:15pm Monday thru Friday, and the same times on Saturday if there was a rainout, during the week.

The games were six inning affairs.

I would have my uniform on by 12:30, right after lunch on game days and be looking for someone to play catch with. If no one was available, I would take a tennis ball and go over to the Canisteo River retaining wall, by the Seneca St. Bridge and practice throwing the ball up against the wall from all angles and catching it. It seemed like I was always trying to get better!

I always felt I was a much better fielder than a hitter.

I was always the first player at Little League Park for our games, and when I wasn't playing Little League games I would be up in the park trying to play baseball with players who were older and much bigger than me.

I was either chosen last or not chosen at all to play with them. I just sucked it up and kept trying!

Although a ton of people had no faith in me, I had plenty of faith in myself, thanks to the Lord for that.

I was totally into baseball, at least until baskeball came along!

Baseball was fun and it kept my mind and body occupied!

I could tell you what all the Major League batting averages were from day to day, along with the home run and RBI leaders. I had just a terrific memory when it came to this sort of thing. Too bad it never spilled over in school.

From 1950 through 1956 I hardly ever missed a home game of the Hornell

Dodgers, a class D farm club of the Brooklyn Dodgers.

It was a gol darn good brand of baseball too. It cost only 25 cents admission for kids and if I didn't have the money to go I would somehow sneak into the park. I was the ultiment fan if there ever was one.

There were times I would be the bat boy for the visiting team and that would get me into the game for free too. Hot dogs were 25 cents and a coke a dime.

Unbelievable compared to the prices of today.

Believe me, those hot dogs were the best ever too.

Listening to all of the Hornell Dodgers away games on the radio was also quite enjoyable, for me..

If there was no game, I would tune in a Major League game.

Willie Mays was my favorite player and he was a dandy! He could do it all!

I loved to listen to his games for you never knew when he would do something outstanding!

The Boston Red Sox were always my team in the American League and remain so today.

When working and living in the Albany, N.Y. area in 1988, I along with another Red Sox fan would get out of work at 3:00pm and we would drive to Boston for a night game. We would have the cah pahked and be in our Fenway Pahk seat by 6:50pm. Leave the Pahk sometime around 10:30pm, getting home around 2:30am. Believe me, 6:00am rolled around awfully quick! I pulled this one trick pony three times and the Sox lost twice, which made for a longer ride or so it seemed! Talk about dedication or determination or maybe a lot of both! When looking back, sometimes maybe a little too much of both !

When I was twelve or thirteen, sometimes I would walk down to Mattie's Ice Cream parlor in Hornell, buy a box of excellent popcorn and sit on the curb and listen to the Hornell Dodgers games on their radio put out on loud speakers.

Todays popcorn could never be classified as excellent.

I once had a signed baseball in my possession that baseball legend Ty Cobb had hit for a home run way back in 1918.

I came by it from my Grandpa Baker's brother Rhile, who lived in Milton Jct., Wisconsin. He had gone to Detroit to see the Tigers and Ty play.

Ty hit a home run and Uncle Rhile caught the ball.

He waited for Ty to shower and dress, catching him when he came outside the park and had him autograph the ball.

This was a rare trophy since Ty hit but 70 some home runs over his entire twenty-two year career. He had a CAREER batting average of .367, and at one time held the career stolen base record. WOW! One of the truly greats of all time to be sure.

Grand Uncle Rhile came east in 1950 to visit my grandpa, when I was ten, and brought the ball as a gift for me. I never realized at the time, just how rare the ball was or what it would represent in monetary value in later years.

I used it just like any another ball when I needed one and lost it somewhere along the way, or during one of our many moves.

That ball today would fetch somewhere between two to three hundred thousand dollars. Boy what an expensive mistake that was.

But at the time I had no way of knowing its true worth.

A Hall of Fame Baseball Connection Lost! ....

In the Spring of 1957, when I was sixteen, soon to be seventeen, I worked part time after school as a janitor at Radio Station WLEA on Mondays, Wednesdays, and Fridays. I also did a fifteen minute sports show at 5:45pm on Saturdays. The owner of the station, Charles (Shot) Henderson asked me if I would like to do live broadcasts of little league games in April and May. He said he would share the proceeds of the commercials with me.

The station would get 67% and I would get 33% of whatever money the commercials brought in! It sure sounded good to me.

People would stop me on the street and tell me what a great job I was doing and how they enjoyed listening to me every afternoon. I received many phone calls from people giving me the same nice compliments.

That was real sweet of them all, my thoughts.

When it came time for splitting up the commercial money, it didn't quite work out the way Shot had told me it would. WLEA made over two thousand dollars and he gave me twenty-five dollars. Thats right $25. He said that was all I needed at my age. I should have made him sign a contract with me in the beginning! I never really expected to get seven hundred dollars, but a couple of hundred would have been nice!

Talk about a royal hosing! My first real experience with greed. Not good!

One Bad Connection Here!.........

Basketball came into the picture for me big time when I tried out for my Bryant Elementary School team in 1951-52. EVERYONE that tried out for the team of 5th and 6th graders made it, just by trying out. There were nineteen boys on that school team, but I wasn't one of them. How could that be possible you ask, if the previous statement I just made was true?

One very simple answer! As a prerequisite for making the team, you had to at least be able to shoot the ball up to the basket. Being so little, I wasn't quite able to accomplish this small feat. All of the kids on the team would laugh at me when I tried. I acted like I didn't hear them, but of course I did.

Six years later there would be no laughs from these nineteen kids!

However, they did let me be part of the team just the same.

I was allowed to sit on the bench in dress clothes for all games, home and away. I just couldn't play.

I loved basketball right from the get-go and once again, I was determined to get better no matter how long it took and/or how tall I ever got.

My good buddy Bob Egan played for the Lincoln School team. He would get a rebound, dribble the length of the court, take a long shot, and quickly get back on defense. He had what we called game! I marveled at how well he played. He was about five inches taller than me!

Could I ever play like him someday, I wondered? I sure hoped so!

It wasn't very long before I got a little bit bigger and a lot more physically mature. I joined my church team, Christ Episcopal in the SSBL, (Sunday School Basketball League) when I was in the 7th grade. At least I was now able to shoot the ball up to the basket.

The were four games played on Wednesday nights at the YMCA from 6:00pm to 10:00pm.

We practiced on Monday nights at the Lincoln Elementary School from 7:00pm to 8:30pm. I lived for the games and even the practices. Little by little, I was getting better. I could just feel it and of course, I wanted more!

All the teams in the league had nice uniforms. All the teams that is, except us! Over the years, prior to my joining the team, our uniforms were either lost, misplaced or outright stolen. One player might have a shirt only, another just shorts, another a full uniform, while another player, (like me) had nothing at all.

I had to wear a white t-shirt and gold trunks, my mom bought me.

I asked the coach about this imposition and he put me off with a weak excuse, that it wasn't up to him. The church was supposed to supply the uniforms. Well yeah, but what if they don't? Shouldn't you bring it to their attention to get some new ones? At the very least try, after all your the adult here, at least I think you are, were my thoughts!

Without any further delay, I decided I would address this problem on my own. I would require no other help in my quest!

Shortly, one night after a game, I noticed the lights were still on at Christ Church, which was located right next door to the YMCA.

Although it was 9:15pm, I decided to drop in and have a talk with Father John Furlong, our Rector, about the uniform crisis we were dealing with!

Father John was putting out candles on the alter and was both startled and surprised to see me sitting in a front row pew, silently watching him go about his business.

Father John was originally from England, by way of Canada but he never lost his English accent.

Peta, What brings you into church at this late hour of the night.?"

"Father John, are you acquainted with the SSBL over at the YMCA?"

"Yes Peta, I most certainly am!"

"Well Father John, our team is in a big bind!" "What kind of a bind Peta?" Every team in the league has nice uniforms except us!" "We might have a pair of pants here, a shirt there or in my case, hardly anything at all!"

"Well Peta, what would you have me do about this problem?"

On the QT, I had already been up to Jacks Sport Shop on Seneca St., and had priced out twelve uniforms. Besides checking out the prices I had also seen what the uniforms would look like, from an available sports catalog.

The uniforms would be bright gold, with purple trim and purple numbers on the back. Across the front in purple lettering would be Christ Episcopal.

"Father, I would like the church to furnish us with some new uniforms."

"Ok Peta, you go up to Jack's Sport Shop and get a price for how many uniforms you will need and come back to me with that information and we'll go from there!"

"Already done Father John!" "Really," a big smile now forming all over his face! "How much?" "Eighty four dollars for twelve uniforms!"

That price would maybe buy one uniform today. Maybe!

After some deep thought, Father John spoke. "Alright Peta, you may go up and order the uniforms, on one condition," You must collect the uniforms after every game, be responsible for them and keep them clean and in good condition."

I agree Father John." "OK Peta, I'm so glad you stopped in, bringing this situation to my attention!" "Me too, Father John, me too"

My feet hardly touched the icy ground on the way home that night.

I recalled ordering two small, five medium and five large uniforms!

That should do it! And it did! My teammates and I were going to have some nice uniforms even if I had to personally take charge to get them.

Grit and Determination had prevailed once again. YES!

A Father John/Peta Connection!..........................

The uniforms, when they came, made us look just as classy as the other seven teams in the league. I never knew for sure if my teammates knew how the new uniforms were acquired, but they sure appreciated getting them.

I told them the church got them for us, but I never mentioned the process it took on my part. I never thought it necessary for me to divulge this information! All of us had a uniform now and thats all that mattered to me!

I played for Christ Church from the seventh through the ninth grade.

One cold, Winter night when I was in the eleventh grade and playing for the high school, I received a phone call from Father John who was at the Y. "Peta, do you have the church's' uniforms?" No Father John I sure don't."

"I haven't played for the team since I started playing for the high school, two years ago."You could only play for one, but not both. I certainly would have, if it was at all possible!

"I gave them to the coach Father, my last game before I went up to the high school to play."

"You told me you would take full responsibility for them when I let you purchase them, do you remember?"

"Yes, I do remember Father John and I did take responsibility for them, while I was playing for the team, but I can't be responsible for them for the rest of my life." "Father, there must have been a turnover of coaches during the last couple of years."

"I'm sorry Father John, but you'll just have to try and track them down." I gave him the name of the last coach I played for and wished him luck in his hunt to find the uniforms!

After an exhaustive search, he finally located them and all was well, once more.

Just so Connections never seem to cease; When Father John retired as Rector, he and his wife moved from the Episcopal Rectory on Genesee St. to an apartment at 113 Maple St, right next door to the home we purchased in the Fall of 1970. While I painted my house in the summer of 1971, he would sit in a lawn chair, drink some wine and give me advice on how to paint the house, among the many other things he advised me on!

He also told me during this time that the adult men were no where near as responsible for handling the Christ Church uniforms as I had been, when I took care of them, as a thirteen year old boy back in the early fifties!..........

Father John would pass away of a stroke in 1977!

In the 11th grade in 1956-57, while playing for the Hornell High JV(Junior Varsity) we lost at Painted Post in our opening game

40-36. I had seventeen points for the game, but It wasn't nearly enough to bridge the four point gap.

It would be the ONLY game we would lose all year.

One game that season stands out big in my memory!

It was our eleventh game of the season.

We were on our bus, on the way to play at Corning Free Academy. Academy along with Corning Northside were our two arch rivals.

One of the Varsity Cheerleaders, Martha Glynn came up to the back of the bus and advised me that Coach O'Neil wanted to see me up in the front of the bus, asap.

At the time I was our leading scorer at almost seventeen points a game and we were riding high with a nine game winning streak. Whatever did coach want to see me about now, my thoughts as I made my way up to the front of the bus! Maybe he wanted to discuss puting a trap press on them from the start or some other strategic plan, such as a certain zone defense, he might have in mind to combat their decided height advantge over us!

As it turned out, it wasn't good news for me! In fact it was like a blow beneath the belt!

"Look Pete, your not going to start tonight." "We're going to play man to man on defense." "Every one of their starters is six feet or taller and your only 5'4." "There's just no one to match you up against on defense because of your height disadvantage."

"Don't be too upset though, since you'll be in the game in a very short time."

"Why don't we play zone, coach?" "Coach Hartman (the varsity coach) wants us to play man, but don't worry you'll be in the game soon enough." "CFA is 9-1 too and we want to win this game some kind of bad."

How in the world do you bench your leading scorer, especially for that reason!? I would call this a bad case of over coaching from a real good coach. I just took a shot to my mid section and Coach O'Neil is telling me not to get too upset. Are you kidding me!

One Real Bad Connection Here!................

Discrimination again. This time for being too gosh darn short.

I myself had been looking forward to this big game for the two weeks leading up to it, and now I wasn't even going to start! Unbelievable!

For sure, this was a a hit to my psyche!

My quickness and speed, coupled with my shooing ability should have carried the day here, compared to any height deficit of eight inches.

I thought, whoever I guarded would not score more points then I would. Guaranteed! End of story! That wasn't how coach O,Neil saw it though, and thats what really mattered!

Maybe Coach Hartman gave Coach O'Neil the order to do this to me, who knows. Hartman, for whatever reason, didn't have much faith in me and because of it, the feeling was mutual from my end too!

This made no sense to me or the rest of my teammates either when they learned the news! After all, here was your leading scorer sitting on the bench!

The game was a nail biter as advertised from beginning to end, with neither team leading at anytime by more than three points until the very end of the game. It was a bitter back and forth affair!

It must have been an exiting game to watch, but for me it sure wasn't, since it felt like I was permanetly glued to the bench.

At the end of three quarters the score was tied at forty-one all, and the Corning crowd was going absolutely crazy.

Over this entire stretch I had not played a lick! It was as if I was being punished for something I had done. The only thing that I had done wrong was being born from short parents!

This was a siuation I had no control over and I had to fight back tears, after all men don't cry! But down deep inside of me I cried!

Believe me, It was one tough experience to go through!

With a little less than two minutes to go in the game and the score still knotted at 51, Corning had the ball out of bounds at side court after a timeout.

At this point Coach O'neill summoned me from the bench and I finally entered the fray.

Now playing the point man in a one-two-two zone, I quickly stole Academys in bound pass and headed for the go ahead basket.

I was fouled hard on the shot attempt, knocking me sprawling face first to the floor, of course missing the basket in the attempt!

Gathering myself up off the floor, I stepped up to the foul line and made both free throws putting us up by two points 53 to 51.

When Academy attempted to bring the ball back down court, once again I swiped another pass and dribbled all over the front court until a CFA player finally caught up with me and once again, fouled me hard from behind.

Once again I made both foul shots increasing our lead to four points, the largest spread in the game!

Time was now running down in our favor!

Academy should have known better than to foul me, but then I never gave them much of a choice!

Once again CFA brought the ball down court, and once again I stole the ball, this time from the dribbler. I dribbled all over the front court with all the CFA players in hot pursuit of me. Just as I was about to be fouled for the third time, with only a few seconds showing on the clock, I flipped the ball up toward the high ceiling. Looking at the nearest Corning player, I spoke out, "When that ball comes down, this game is over!" The ball came down, the buzzer sounded before it hit the floor and the game was indeed over!

We walked away with a big 55-51 win, especially away from home!

Whenever sports intangibles are discussed, always remember this about the heart and soul of any player, in any sport, in any game. Its so much larger than just SIZE ALONE. So much more so, that it can't be truly defined.

Maybe the best way to put it would be this; Its not always the size of the dog in the fight, but the size of the fight in the dog!

Moving ahead to my senior year. I wasn't a starter. I didn't even play very much although everyone on the team knew I should be starting or at the very least playing a heckuva lot more than I was. Everyone, that is, except Coach Hartman.

During the Christmas break of 1957 we had a full court scrimmage with Canisteo High, five miles down the road, on their home court. We were class AA and they were class A.

I knew the rims on their backboards were very tight, which meant it was harder to make baskets with no play in the rim. You had to swish every shot, since you got no help from the rims. With rims that wern't so tight, you could now and then get a friendly bounce or roll on a shot that wasn't dead on.

Sometimes the ball would bounce around the window (backboard) and/or the rim and go in!

Knowing this about their rims showed just how much I was into basketball!

There wan't much in baseball or basketball, that I didn't observe!

Canisteo had an excellent team, winning eighteen straight games during the regular season before losing their first and only game in the A Division of the State Sectional Playoffs. During the scrimmage, my best bud, Bob Egan was goofing around so Hartman pulled him and inserted me in his place.

In around four minutes, I scored eight baskets in eight attempts.

There were two long set shots, two long jump shots, a runner in the lane and three steals all for for baskets, and all of the swish variety!

More than excellent by any standard of basketball!

After my last steal and basket, the scrimmage was mutually called off.

I remember the look on some of their players faces, wondering what had just hit them! Their coach, Mark Meck ran up to me, got me in a neck hold and said this, "I've been around basketball for over twenty-five years and I've never seen anything like what I just saw you do." He added that if I moved to Canisteo, I could start for his team this coming Friday night. Knowing this wasn't even a remote possibility, I said "Yeah, right!"

After the scrimmage, Alan Stook, one of our best players came up to my locker in the dressing room, towel in hand and said, "If Hartman doesn't come in here and tell you your starting Friday, I am going to eat this towel, right here and now!"" "You better find some salt or pepper Stookie, because It's not going to taste very good," was my candid reply!

All my other teammates were also cloistered around my locker waiting to hear what Hartman had to say about what had just taken place.

Hartmans exact words to me were; "Well Pete if you keep playing like you did out there today, I'm going to have to find some playing time for you!"

Quite unbelievable, but it was just about what I expected him to say, if he said anything at all, which was also quite possible too!

Hartman had a chance after this outstanding performance to make amends for his cockeyed position to not play me much and he completely blew it. He would feel its sting two months later against Corning Northside on Feb 27th, 1958.

Stook threw the towel up in the air and walked away in disgust!

The rest of the players now dispersed, shaking their heads in disbelief too.

I had no knowledge of it at the time, but I played this scrimmage with a broken right foot bandaged with only an ACE bandage!...I had hurt it a few days earlier in the month, one afternoon in practice. I knew it hurt a lot but never knew at the time, it was broken! I just tightly taped it up tight for games and practice and played through it, pain and all!

I found out in late January of 1961 that it had been broken sometime in December of 1957. Unbelievable, but it had healed perfectly! With no cast either! However It did take six months to fully heal without a cast!

Much more about this incident in the chapter of Dr. James R. Kelly, Part II!

Once again, you can't make this stuff up!

Although I was the best shot on the team, I was always the first one on the court for practice and the last one to leave.

We each had to shoot twenty five foul shots at the end of every practice with the player going next feeding the shooter.

I always chose go last which made Hartman feed me. He hated it! I always took my time shooting a foul shot and wouldn't deviate from it even in practice! If I made twenty five straight, I would shoot until I missed!

One afternoon I was fifty for fifty. Hartman wanted to call it off at that point and go home. I said no way, maybe I could be 100 for 100 and talked him into letting me finish. I didn't miss until my 73rd attempt. I talked him into letting me shoot until I missed again, which I did on my 95th attempt. I finished making 98 out of 100.

Whenever I stepped up to that line it was as automatic as anything in sports could be! Practice makes perfect or so they say! I was an excellent example of that!

Classes let out at 3:15pm and we didn't have to be on the court for practice until 4:00pm. I was always there by 3:30pm at the very latest. Practice days were Monday, Wednesday and Thursday, with games on most Tuesdays and Fridays, and one or two games on a Saturday.

After supper on Monday and Thursday I would play with my age group at the YMCA from 7:00pm until 8:30.

More often then not, I would then stick around and play with the men from 8:30 until 10:00 if they didn't have enough players to make up two or three teams.

One night when I was fifteen, while playing with the men at the Y, I stole the ball from Cy McCormick, who was twenty-three. When attemting the ensuing layup, he ran me hard into the wall and glowered over me on the floor, while at the same time, saying thats what would happen again if I stole another ball from him. Since I was a hard nosed competitor and wouldn't back down from anyone, I stole it from him once again and this time feinted him out. After he flew past me, I layed it up and in.

After the night was over he came up to me in the shower and apologized for the hard hit he had put on me and congratulated me for faking him out the second time! Alls well that ends well, I guess.

I would be at the Y on some Saturday mornings or afternoons just for shooting practice. Of course I would play at different courts out doors in the heat, cold, snow or rain. Sometimes we would have to shovel snow a foot deep off the court, just to be able to play. Or maybe chip ice an inch thick. Grit and determination on display here!

The only thing that slowed me down at all was if the temperature reached 10 degrees or lower. When the temperature reached this low, you couldn't feel the ball to shoot and you had to feel the ball to be able to do that much!

As a sophomore, I was once barred from the YMCA for two weeks, for sneaking into the Y on a cold Sunday to shoot baskets. There was supposed to be no activity of any kind at the Y on Sundays. YMCA stood for Young Mens Christian Associan.

Looking back, I was 100% wrong. I shouldn't have snuck on that Sunday, but the temperature outside was eight below zero and shooting baskets is not conducive to your fingers or other body parts when it's that gosh darn cold.

I didn't want to do anything bad, just shoot baskets!

I played basketball off and on, right up to the age of sixty-two or until I ran out of places to play and/or people to play with! I also took up running at age fifty two and ran until I was sixty three!

There was a foul shooting contest nationwide in the spring and I was determined to win the trophy that was in Dee's Diamonds Jewelry store window on Main St., all Winter long. After all I was a 90% plus foul shooter so I figured it wouldn't be much of a stretch to win this nice trophy.

I checked the trophy out every time I passed by Dee's window and I passed by there at least once or twice every day. Much More about this later, after the last game of my high school career!

Hornell and the two Corning schools (Northside and Free Academy) all finished in a three way tie for the right to represent Steuben County in the AA Division of the State Sectional Playoffs at Rochester, N.Y. We each won at home and lost on the road to each other, finishing at 2-2.

There would have to be a two game playoff to determine which team would be going to the state playoff. Academy drew a bye so it was us against Northside on Thursday, February 27 at a neutral site, Bath, N.Y.

The winner would face Academy on Saturday at Bath with the winner of that game going on to the State Sectionals.

We led Northside at halftime by five points. I had not been in the game.

At the half time shoot a round I couldn't miss. Everything I shot went in. From any distance too! I sure had a hot hand. I could just feel it! If only I could get in the game! Boy, could I ever help the team out tonight if only I could get the chance, my thoughts!

Northside caught us midway through the third quarter, went ahead and never looked back. I never got in the game and we lost by nine points.

At the end of the third quarter I told Hartman if he wanted to win this important game, he needed to put me in, and he needed to do it right away.

I told him, "I've only got eight minutes left to turn this thing around!"

He just waved me off, and said; "You don't have any idea at all of what your talking about."

I did know what I was talking about and in a little more then twenty four hours Hartman would find out the hard way just how right I was!

He was about to be hit with a whirlwind and he never saw it coming!

To be honest, neither did I.

Here was a man with little or no faith in me, but one that would have his thinking tipped upside down and sideways, before the next night was in the history books! Hartman had thrown me under the bus on this night!

The next night, much to his chagrin, I would be driving the bus!

It was a short bus ride home that Thursday evening, but it seemed like an eternity for me, knowing that I could have helped us win the game, if I had only been given the opportunity to do so! If only.........

Sleep for me, of course would not come! Not on this night anyways!

Another Bad Basketball Connection....................

The next night was Friday, February 28, 1958. It was senior night and since I was a senior, I would be starting the game against St. Anthony of Padua of Watkins Glen, N.Y. in our final game of the season.

I recall it was a balmy evening for the time of year with a temperature right around 50 degrees.

In the team huddle before the game, I said a little prayer that no one on either side would get hurt, and hopefully we five seniors would play well enough to win our last game. The last game we five would ever play for HHS! A little sad for me, but the end was near!

Hopefully Lord, maybe I could score in double figure's for the game. This might help me prove what I could really do if I ever had been given a fair chance from the beginning! My thoughts anyways.

If I could do this, it would prove that I deserved to be starting or playing a lot more instead of just taking up space on the bench.

Never in my wildest dreams did I ever envision what was about to take place on what turned out to be one exiting night for our team and a special one for me.

I was about to be rewarded big time for all the years of hard work and dedication I had put in to get to this point in time.

If not for my girlfriend, I might never have been in this position. Although I was never a quitter, more then once I thought about leaving the team because I wasn't playing much at all. I felt humiliated because in my heart of hearts, I knew I should be playing a whole lot more than I was! It was eating me up inside.

I knew deep down she thought I was good enought to play regardless, and that meant the world to me. I wish I had told her about all of this, but of course, I never did..

Problems of the heart don't always work out well for males. Why do we always think we have to tough everything out by ourselves? Even when we're getting knocked from piller to post!

I guess we don't want to look like losers, at least not to special people we care about.

And because I didn't want to look like a quitter, especially a quitter in her eyes of all people, I quietly tried to hang in there! Not an easy thing to do under such tough conditions!

So many things you wished you had said when you were younger and didn't say and so many things you did say, that you wished you hadn't said or could retract. Spilled milk does not go back easily in the bottle. In fact It doesn't go back at all! I guess we all come under this large umbrella from time to time. No one more than me!

Karma would find me big time before this night was over!

I had five baskets for ten points in the opening quarter and we led 29-20. Double figures already. Not bad for a bench warmer, my thoughts.

Most important though, we were winning and firing on all cylinders as a team! At the half we were up by twenty one points 49-28. I had sixteen points, on eight field goals, along with a slew of steals and assists!

With two minutes left in the third quarter, Hartman for some unknown reason, brought me to the bench.

It certainly wasn't my decision! And I sure didn't need any rest either!

At this point I had ten baskets for twenty points and we still led by the comfortable margin of twenty-one points.

With only six minutes left in the game, Padua had cut into our once insurmountable lead and now trailed us by just nine points, 75-66.

The crowd was getting anxious! "We want Babcock, we want Babcock," came their loud chant.

Back in the game I came. I was on a mission now, so look out!

In rapid sucession, I hit three quick baskets; a long jump shot from the corner, another jump shot from the top of the key and I drained a long thirty five foot set shot. Two free throws. Next came a steal and another basket. We were off to the races once again, and won going away by twenty four points, 96-72.

We were outshot percentage wise 54% to 44%, but still won by 24 points.

Go figure that one!

I had 16 baskets, four free throws for a total of 36 points for the game!

My girlfriends telephone number back then, was 1636J! Some kind of surreal Connection there, don't you think?

You can't make this stuff up!

One Pretty Surreal Connection Here!..........

I ended up the night with eleven steals and ten assists plus the thirty six points, one point shy of our school single game scoring record at the time. Some more significant highlights of the big game!

No one mentioned it but the sixteen baskets, I believe were a one game record at HHS then and maybe still are to this day.

They didn't count assists and steals in high school games back then, but I counted them myself. To me they were just as important as points scored and they most absolutely were!.......

I had a triple double a long time before that moniker was ever coined!

If we had had the three point arc back in the 50's I would have had 46 points, because ten of my basket's were from well beyond that distance!

In the last six minutes of the game I scored sixteen points. Not bad for someone not good enough to play even a minute the night before!

Quite Unbelievable!

After a timeout ended midway through the fourth quarter, Hartman grabbed me by one arm and wanted me to basket hang under our basket(not go back and play defense) so I could break the one game record.

Here's a coach who didn't think I was even good enough to play one night earlier, and now he wanted me to do something, which I thought was quite unethical the next night. Just to break a record. I don't think so!

No way I wanted any part of that scheme, my thoughts!

I yelled back at him, saying I would break the record on the up and up or I wouldn't break the record at all! Good for you Pete, my thoughts!

Egan, my perpetual buddy winked at me as if to say, right on Pete!

I didn't break the record that night but I played the game my way, and proved my point three fold that I truly belonged in the starting lineup!

I've run this around in my mind many times in the last half century.

I think Hartman may have gotten caught up in the excitement of the moment, like everyone else. So I have given him a free pass on this one!

However, he did tell me in the locker room after the game that he had made a big mistake with me. Really coach? Really?, my thoughts.

Way too late for that coach. That train left the station a long time ago.

In fact It left during the Christmas break,way back in December at Canisteo!

If my performance in that full court scrimmage didn't open his eyes, there was absolutely nothing else I could possibly do that would, my thoughts!

Without any doubt, I know I could have helped our team out the night before against Northside! I think the outcome would have had a far different ending if I had played. When I was on a roll, there was no stopping me, my height of 5' 4" withstanding unless I was fouled and since I was deadly at the foul line, that wouldn't stop me either!

Funny thing about athletes. Some need a pat on the back while others need a kick in the rear. I was one that needed someone to show some faith and respect me for my abilities and not judge me by my small stature alone.

Not asking much there. Neither did I ever get from Hartman.

I may have been small in size, but I sure came up big when the chips were down! I'm sorry Hartman had to find this out, the hard way!

When someone believed in me, I would go through a brick wall for them or die trying! I guess even if they didn't show faith in me, I would still try. Nuff said!

A Happy Connection, One Night After A Disappointing One!...................……

As a nice note of interest; My mom and Grandma Baker were at my big game so it was that much nicer for me too. They never told me they were coming, they just showed up, which was a sweet surprise! I wish my father had been there too but of course, that was just wishful thinking on my part……..............

I vividly remember where my girlfriend was sitting by the stairs to the gym and that she was wearing a green short sleve sweater and brown slacks!

Looking back on everything, It was one surreal night. It was like my game had been elevated to a much higher level, and maybe it had, on that special night so long ago! I always knew I could play like this, but to play this well even suprised the daylights out of me!

Of the nineteen kids from that Bryant Elementary School team, six years before, when I wasn't big enough to play with them, not one of them was even on that high school varsity team with me.

I'm sure there wasn't any laughing now! At least none directed my way!

What you can accomplish with a ton of grit, determination and literally years of dedicated practice. If you stay the course, more times than not, you will be justly rewarded no matter what! Thank you Lord for your faith in me!

One Important Connection Finally Made!.............

I still had a foul shooting contest to win, remember!

The foul shooting contest which was nationwide, was held locally in different age groups. My age group was age fifteen to twenty.

Teammate Stook and I tied, each making twenty-two of twenty-five shots or 88%. Pretty good, in any league, however, the best was yet to come.

On one Saturday afternoon in late March, I was all alone shooting baskets at the YMCA. By this time the trophy had now been moved from the jewelry store window, down to the YMCA counter under glass.

Bob Griswold, the Athletic Director at the Y walked into the gym.

"Hey Pete, don't you and Stook have to have a fifty shot shoot off for the trophy that's under glass, out in the lobby?" "Yeah Griz, we sure do." "You want to shoot your fifty Pete?" "I'll feed you and also be your witness."

"Sounds good to me Griz, lets do it!"

Buckle up your seat belts for this one!

I made forty seven out of fifty foul shots or 94%, almost unbeatable or so Griz thought. To be quite honest, I thought so too. It would be extremely hard to beat this performance, my thoughts! Griz said he would be right back. "Where are you going anyways?" "I'm going to call the Tribune (our local newspaper) to come over and take your picture with the trophy."

"Hold on Griz, not so fast, you can't do that." "After all, Stookie hasn't shot yet." "You're right Pete, but do you really think he can possibly beat you now?" "No I don't, but he's sure going to get his chance!"

Later, when Stook finally shot his fifty, he didn't make forty seven, he made forty eight or 96%. There went my trophy. The trophy I coveted so much went right down the drain. Congrats to Stookie!

A Teammate Connection!..........

There was one other game I vividly remember my senior year.

It was at Batavia, N.Y., on our first game back in early January, right after the Christmas break.

This was the game that Stook said I should be starting after my unreal shooting display in the scrimmage at Canisteo.

The Blue Devils from Batavia led us by twenty-one points at halftime. One of their players made a three point play to start the third quarter and we were down 43 to 19, away from home, to boot. One tough mountain to climb for sure! Although I didn't play in the first half, I started and played the entire second half. I only scored nine points, but I had eight steals and nine assist's for the half! Not a bad all around performance, all things considered!

Little by little we climbed out of that black hole, right back into this tough game and unbelievable as it may seem, we finally caught the Devils and tied them at 58 all!

Big MO (MOMENTUM) was on our side big time in this huge and unlikely comeback! The look on the Batavia players faces told the whole story. How was it humanly possible that you guys could have caught us, down twenty four points and away from home for sauce! We definitely had them hanging on the ropes now! If only we could just somehow put them away!

At this juncture in the game, Stook and I commited costly turnovers and we eventually lost this heart-rending game 63-60, but what a great comeback it was! This game showed the true character we possesed! We certainly didn't go quietly into the night! Not on this night anyways! Far from it! We played our hearts out in this hard fought game, only to lose. This was the type of game you could lose, but walk off the court with your head held high. We left everything we had on the court. No one could ask for anything more!

Wouldn't that have been a great game to have won! I would have gladly swapped my big game for a win in this one terrific game.

I think the outcome here would have been far different had I played in the first half! I'll change that THINK statement to KNOW!!

One Tough Connection Here!.............

As an adult, I managed a Little League Baseball team from 1964 thru 1970, and coached a B League Basketball team on Saturday mornings at the YMCA.

I along with two other fathers, Ed Gillette and Don Canty took our little league team to Pittsburg in July of 1970 to see a three game series between the Pirates and the San Francisco Giants.

Every one had a great time and a vacation that no one would ever forget. Many years later The boys, who were now men, would walk up to me on the street and tell me what a fun time they had on that trip, thanking me for making it happen.

Sure, it was my idea, but I had a lot of help from the two fathers.

Great kids they were too! Sad to say, but a couple of those kids (men) have since passed away. Also Ed and Don who went with us are both gone now!

I refereed high school basketball games for twelve years between 1963 and 1975. During that time I also volunteered my referee services to the SSBL every Wednesday night at the YMCA. I worked at least two games a night, sometimes three and a couple of nights four.

One night I worked three games and had to work the fourth game by myself. I remember being so tired after that last game was over, I could hardly crawl into or out of the shower. Worst of all I had to go and work my job on the railroad at midnight. Thank God, it was a desk job!

I missed only ONE night in the twelve years I volunteered my services to the YMCA. One Dedicated Connection Here!...........

Hey, I played in this league years ago, remember.

It sure didn't hurt me to pay back!

Forever Connected With The Kids!.............

One cold Winter night in February of 1973, I got a call from my buddy John Todd, the President of the SSBL. He refereed games when I played in the league and also games when I played for the high school. He was the person who got me interested in becoming a referee, in the first place.

"Pete, I need a big favor from you and I won't take no for an answer!" "Ok, John, what's up?" "Christ Episcopal's coach has up and quit and I can't seem to find anyone interested in coaching the team for the remaining seven games of the season."

"Father John said something about you owing him on account of some uniforms from a couple of years back." " Good Lord John, nineteen years ago to be exact, when I was just a boy of thirteen!"

"Well anyways, he said to ring you up and ask you, so will you fill in as the interem coach for these last seven games?"

"I would really like to help both you and Father John out, but how can I both coach and referee in the league at the same time?"

"Big conflict of interest here, don't you think, my friend?"

"The seven other coach's would have kittens and you should know that, way better then me." "I can just see Joe Murray(St.

Ignatius) and Lyle Westcott(Park Methodist) right now." "There would be pure bedlem!"

"Look Pete, everyone knows how honest you are, will you do this as a special favor to me and Father John if I can get at least a majority of the coach's to go along?" Thinking this idea would never take flight in a million years, I answered in the affirmative.

"I'll call you up tomorrow night Pete, with the results."

John called me up the next evening and said Congratulations, it's a done deal. I was now the new coach of Christ Church for the remaining seven games, and I could also continue to referee.

"How many arms did you have to twist on this one John?"

"None, the coaches voted seven to zero for it."

So I both refereed and coached for the remaining seven games of the season. Unheard of in this league or any other league for that matter too!

Once again, you can't make this stuff up!!!

Some of those coaches knew me when I played there many years ago.

Most when I reffed there and now when I also coached there too!

I guess what goes round, always comes back around again!

Don't you just love the Connections when they ALL come together!

A Player/ Referee/Coach Connection Finally Made!.............

MR. ERIE

Mr. Leo Mathews was called Mr. Erie for a reason and sometimes a not to affectionate reason it was either. He was the Chief Clerk to the Trainmaster and the Road Foreman of Engineers for the Erie Railroad. These two men were the supervisors for all the trainmen and enginemen that operated out of the Hornell Terminal. Needless to say, they held very prestigious positions on the railroad. Mr. Mathews ran a tight ship and watched out for these men one hundred and twenty five per cent. Nobody and I mean nobody, got to see either of them except through Mr. Mathews.

I always called him Mr. Mathews until later when I got to know him much better, but that would be a few years and a few tears down the road.

I respected Mr. Mathews, not only for his position, but also for the way he handled his job. He was like a top Sargent in the Army. I was only interested in getting a decent job. Needless to say, I wasn't having any luck at all.

Uncle Carl, my mothers oldist brother, worked as a trainman on the Lehigh Valley Railroad out of Buffalo, N.Y. He pulled some strings and got me a job as a trainman in the summer of 1958. I couldn't pass the physical because I wore glasses. Discrimination again, this time just for wearing glasses. This would never fly today. Surely, not for that reason anyways, unless I totally refused to wear them, but remember this was 1958.

My first encounter with Mr. Mathews was sometime in October of 1959 when I went into his office at the Erie Railroad Depot in Hornell.

All I wanted to do was to make out an application for employment with the railroad. I would take any job that was available. I just wanted a job!

Each time I went there, I was always dressed real nice with dress pants, a white shirt, a cardigan sweater and shoes that were all shined up.

He took one look at me and asked me my name. "Peter Babcock." "Babcock, you already have an application on file and besides, we're not hiring in any department at the present time." "I've never been in this office before, Mr. Mathews." "Take my word for it Babcock, you have been here and already have an application on file with us." "This is the first time I've been in this office, Mr. Mathews, please believe me." "Trust me Babcock, you have been here before and you have made out an application." "Besides, we're not hiring anyway!"

I turned and left, quite puzzled as any one would be, under this set of circumstances.

I decided to try again in early January of 1960. This time Mr. Mathews took one look at me and asked what I was doing back there again. "I would just like to make out an application for employment." "That's all I want to do." I was trying hard to be persistent without being a nuisance.

Under the conditions, It was becoming awfully hard to manage!

"Babcock, I have already told you once that you have an application on file, so please leave and don't ever come back in here again."

I had to pass the Road Foreman's office on my way out and the RFE, P.R. Frisbee stopped me by the door and asked me my name. When I told him, he asked me if Cliff Babcock, a trainman, was my father. I will say, my father had a good record as an employee. I nodded yes. "How would you like to hire out as a fireman on a diesel engine?" "Would I ever." was my quick reply "Leo, come in

here with an application form and also a physical request form too."
Mr. Mathews grudgingly brought the forms in as requested, but, he
wasn't happy about it, not at all, as the frown on his face showed!

After filling out the application, I was then advised to take the
physical form down to the diesel shop hospital where a doctor would
give me a physical. The Doctor turned out to be Dr. Raymond Kelly,
Doctor James Kelly's Father. Dr. Raymand was retired but still did
physicals for the Erie Railroad. Small world, but Dr. Jim would play
a huge role in my life, a little over eight months in the future!

I passed the physical with flying colors, except it was pending
word back from railroad headquarters in Cleveland. Once again
because of the fact, I wore eye glasses.

If you were already working on the railroad in the operating
department and needed glasses that was ok, but they would not hire
you off the street for the road if you wore them. No difference than
the Lehigh Valley. Go figure.

Mr. Mathews took one look at my physical results and a big
smile formed all around his face. Something I didn't quite realize
or connect with, but something he sure knew. He said he would
call me when the results came back from Cleveland in about five to
seven days.

About a week later, Mr. Mathews called me up early one morning
to tell me that he had word back from Cleveland. I could not be
considered for employment as a fireman because of the glasses. He
seemed real happy about it too. Why he seemed so happy about it,
I couldn't figure out because I had never done anything to him to
warrant this kind of treatment.

On the contrary, I had been very polite and cordial. "What
recourse do I have Mr. Mathews?"

"None at all Babcock." "And please do me a big favor and not
come in here anymore either." He than hung up in my ear, without
even saying goodbye. What a bummer this turned out to be!

One Bad Mathews/Babcock Connection!................

In early February I got a call one morning about 7:30am from one of my best friends, (Bill Crowe) father, Francis Crowe. Francis was the General Yardmaster of the rail yards, another highly regarded position that carried a lot of weight on the railroad too. "Pete, how would you like a job on the railroad?" "I sure would Francis!"

He told me to be at Mr. Mathews office at 10:00am and I would be hired on the spot as a clerk if that was ok with me, which it surely was. Wearing glasses wouldn't come into play for this job, he remarked in closing.

My Grandmother Baker had gone behind my back and asked for his help. She never told me about it, until many years later. I guess I should have asked him sooner instead of fighting this abomination on my own.

How she found out about Mr. Crowe, I never knew and it's too late to ask her now. Since I was like another son to him, he told her he would be more then glad to help me get a job with the railroad. "I must tell you Francis, Mr. Mathews has already given me the heave-ho out of his office, twice already." "Well he won't this time, just be there at 10:00am and don't be late."

"I'll be hanging around the trackside of the depot, so when you are finished, come and see me." "I'll be there, right at ten if not before, Francis and thank you for your help, I really appreciate it."

When I walked into Mr. Mathew's office for the third time, at 9:55am he asked me what on earth I was doing there once more. I thought oh boy, here we go again. "Mr. Crowe sent me, Mr. Mathews." "I don't care if President Eisenhower sent you, we're not hiring." "As a clerk," I replied. " We're not hiring in that department or any other department for that matter!"

"That's it, so leave and please don't ever come back in here again."

This time I walked out more discouraged than ever. I walked around the corner of the depot pondering my next move, if there was a next move and there was Francis and Billy standing together by the tracks. Francis yelled out, "How did you make out with Leo?"

"Not good Francis, he threw me out of his office, yet again, for the third time." "Pete, you wait right here with Bill, I'll be right back."

With that he went into Mr. Mathews office. After what seemed like an eternity, but was only about ten minutes, he came out and took me over to the Erie Freight House next to the depot and on the way, told me I was going to be hired on as a clerk through the Freight House instead of the Trainmasters office.

What a terrible ordeal, this whole process had been, but I was finally going to be hired out on the railroad. Lets hear it for grit and persistence!

Mr. Leo Mathews, if he had anything to say about it and for whatever reason was not going to hire me and that was it, no ifs, ands or buts about it.

Leo always went to 11:00 Mass on Sundays at St. Ann's Church. Afterwards, he would stop by the baggage room at the west end of the depot, pick up all the train crews time slips, that had accumulated there over the weekend. He would then take them down to his office at the east end of the depot and work on them for about two hours. He would do this every Sunday, just like clockwork. He was so dedicated to the company and his job, I don't think he even put in the extra pay for doing it.

This may seem real hard to comprehend, but by now Leo and I were pretty good friends, on a first name basis! I called him Leo instead of Mr. Matthews and he called me Petey instead of Babcock.

I would always have the time slips unfolded and sorted for him in each pile that he liked them in. Yellow slips for enginemen, green slips for trainmen, white slips for yardmen and pink slips for everyone who was on vacation.

I would then put a thick rubber band around the whole pile for him.

He once told me no one ever bothered to take the time to do this for him over the years except me and how much he appreciated this little gesture, since it made his job so much easier and quicker too!

The colors of the timeslips reminded me of the color of Monopoly money.

One Sunday after Mass in July of 1967, the following conversation between Leo and I took place. "Good morning Petey, what kind of mood are you in today?" "I'm in the same kind of mood that I'm in most every day Leo, which is good." "Why Leo, what's up today?" "Petey, do you remember a few years back, when you tried to hire out on the old Erie a number of times, and I gave you a real hard time each and every time?" "Yes Leo, of course I remember!"

"Well you turned out to be one cracker jack of an employee and I want to apologize to you and tell you how sorry I am for that harsh and regrettable treatment I put you through back then." "Hey Leo, we all make mistakes, probably no one more than me!" "No Petey, this was very wrong of me and I want to apologize for it!" "Apology accepted Leo, but definitely not needed."

"Yes it is Petey."

Leo was in the confessional box now and he wasn't in any hurry to leave!

""I was wrong to treat you so bad and I'm so sorry for it." It's ok Leo, its ok."

"And I want to tell you the reason why I gave you such a hard time too."

"Its really not nessary Leo." "Yes it is Petey!"

"I thought that L.I. Babcock was your father." " Babcock was a yard brakeman who often took calls and never showed up for work." "Or sometimes he would show up for work real late or mark off after being at work a short time." "Just the name Babcock, made me cringe."

"We didn't want another Babcock around here to give us any more trouble, and needlessly costing us a lot of money."

66

Discrimination once again. This time for not being too short, wearing glasses, or not being the managers son, but just for having a wrong last name, my thoughts!

"Leo, please believe me, it's water long over the falls." " It never even enters my mind." "Really it doesn't, and as far as I am concerned, it never happened!" "In fact, I'm always glad to see you on Sundays, Leo." "I'm sure glad to see you on Sundays too Petey, in fact I look forward to it." "Well thank you Leo, I do appreciate that!"

Looking back, I think the ugly treatment that Leo had given me so long ago, had been on his conscience for quite some time now, along with his need to apologize to me for it, bless his heart.

Maybe it was the homily at Mass this Sunday or whatever, but he had made up his mind to finally do it. He was going to get it off of his chest once and for all and today was going to be that day. I think the fact that he didn't apologize sooner, was his big fear, (the fear that most of us have) that I might not accept his heart felt apology. If this was the case, Leo was badly mistaken, for I was never a person to hold a grudge towards anyone!

And also the fact that I both liked and respected Leo a lot to boot. Even after all the bad treatment he had given me!

I know that Leo and I both felt a whole lot better about things after he left the baggage room that Sunday morning. Needless to say, I had to wipe away a few tears and grab some kleenix to blow my nose after he was out of sight.

I wouldn't let on to Leo, but it had hurt me quite a bit at the time, for I had done nothing wrong to warrant such harsh treatment. I only wanted a job.

Just one more person, who at one time had little or no faith in me, but who now had a much different opinion!

Deja vu all over again!

After becoming good friends with Leo, all the bad memories of those long ago times had vanished completely until he called them forth once again on that Sunday morning!

I really did appreciate Leo's apology though, way more than I let on or he ever realized!

Who would have thought seven years ago, this kind of discussion would ever have taken place, unh?

Finally A Leo/Petey Connection!................

At the end of his life, Leo died one night, unexpectedly in his sleep.

I attended his wake and his funeral at St.Anns.

No way to make this stuff up!

ONCE A RAILROAD TOWN

To me there is something quite nostalgic about a railroad, any railroad!

Where there once was nothing but a field, forest, or stream, there is now two shiny rails, separated only by 4' 8" and ½ inches." Whenever one notices a railroad track, it seems like it has been there forever. But of course it hasn't. Before railroads came on the scene, sometime in the early to mid 1800's, passengers could only move by stage coach, canal or horseback.

A trip today from San Diego to Los Angeles by Amtrak or automobile takes a little less than three hours, but it took a full twenty four hours by stagecoach. And not a smooth ride, it was either. Probably the first words out of the passenger's mouths on their arrival were; I'm so gosh darn tired and my rear end is so sore from all that bouncing around!

And maybe, not in that order either!

Freight could only move by horse or oxen drawn freight wagons, canal boats or primitive ocean going ships.

A railroad today can move a ton of freight, per mile, a heck of a lot cheaper than a truck. Besides, it can move a whole lot more freight, while at the same time, using a whole lot less fuel!.

There was something that touched ones heart and soul when a steam engine's whistle sounded. Two long, one short and another long was one mournful sound...........

The sound would reverberate, deep into ones soul. Especially at night!

There was something about the night, that made it sound even sadder!

Don't ask me why, but there definitely was somehing!

If the wind was just right, you could hear this soul catcher from miles away too. It might be faint, but you could still hear her.

It was a statement by the engine, to let one and all know that she was coming. So get out of her way. She's coming from afar and she'll be leaving soon, once again for far off places.

The air horn of today's diesels pierces the day or night with the same two long blasts, one short and another extra long blast. It is nowhere near as mournful as a steam engine's whistle, but it still speaks a sound of its own.

There is hardly anything worse than when a railroad entirely departs the scene. It is a sadness of the heart, of what once was there and now is no more. It is almost as heartbreaking as a death in the family.

Believe me, railroad people are family. Most of us watched out for each other, sometimes to the detriment of our own selves!

Hornell was at one time a large railroad town. Large would be an understatement of the fact. HUGE would be more like it!

Where there once was two main tracks through town along with a huge rail yard, and all its accoutrements; such as steam/diesel engine shops, a freight transfer house, icing facilities, storehouse and all that remains today is the depot. The depot is now part museum, part doctors offices.

Everything else, is all gone forever. Only one main track survives for a Norfolk Southern or Candian Pacific train, now and then to pass through town.

Whenever talk got around to the Erie or Erie Lackawanna Railroad as it became after the merger in October of 1960, Hornell's part in it would always be a hot topic of discussion. The population of

Hornell in 1940 was around 18,500. Today it would be somewhere around 8,000, maybe even a little less!

The railroad at one time was by far the biggest employer for Hornell and the surrounding area.

Hornell sat at the junction of the Susquehanna, Alleghany and Buffalo Divisions of the Erie Railroad. There were three control towers in Hornell.

They were located at Cass St., Taylor St., and ZY tower. ZY was located at the east end of the eastbound and westbound yards.

Grandmother Baker knew a certain chief train dispatcher, in the train dispatching office that was going to help me get hired out as a tower operator. It was supposidly all but a done deal!

It never happened, because the man (Guy Stewart) retired in 1957, the year before I graduated from high school in 1958.

So that opportunity went flying bye-bye, right out the window!

Much, more about Guy Stewart in a later chapter. In fact thirteen years later in 1970, when the Connection between us would cross paths once again.

This time, we would be neighbors, with Guy's life hanging in the balance.

A failed early Connection between us would end up being,

A Life Saving Connection Thirteen Years Later!................

The Accounting Bureau(Payroll Dept.) for the entire railroad was located in Hornell too, and at one time employed between 200 to 250 people.

There was a huge back shop where the heavy repairs for the steam engine's on the entire railroad were made. Probably close to 1500 men or more were employed there, at one time.

Starting in the mid to late 1950's, when the diesels came on line 100%, there was a drastic cut in the labor force of the shop people by about two-thirds. There was a main storehouse for the entire system and a freight transfer house that employed close to 100 men at one time.

The Susquehanna Division office and train dispatching offices, along with the crew dispatchers were located throughout the depot. A rough guess would be 85 to 100 people who were employed in the depot alone.

Another 250-300 people were employed as yardmasters, clerks, switchmen, enginemen along with car inspectors in the eastbound, westbound and hump yards which included the car repair shops.

Eighteen to twenty one switch engine's per day patrolled the three classification yards, even as late as 1960, when I hired out!

It was the home terminal for the enginemen and trainmen that manned the trains for the Alleghany and Buffalo Divisions, west out of Hornell and the Susquehanna & Scranton Divisions to the east. In later years, Hornell would also be the away from home terminal for crews from Scranton, Buffalo, Meadville, Pa. and Port Jervis, N.Y.

A rough guess would be another 500 plus total employees, in this capacity.

There were stock pens where livestock were unloaded, fed and watered every 36 hours, while in transit, then reloaded back in stock cars for further moves to eastern markets. There was a large icing facility to ice cars with perishable freight, such as meat, oranges, lemons, cherries, lettuce, celery, etc., coming from the west and headed to eastern markets in New England and New York.

All these employee's were paid very well, along with the best of benefits. By 1960 the railroad in Hornell was almost as big of an operation as it was in 1940. That is except for the death of the steam engine, which lopped off hundred's of jobs in the steam engine back shops.

The diesels required periodic maintenance alright, but no wheres near what the steam engines had once demanded.

I considered myself quite fortunate to have become employed by the Erie Railroad in early February of 1960. I posted (railroad lingo for training) for two weeks with Jeff Morris, who was a peach of a man. Jeff was one of the nicest men I ever had the privilege of knowing and over the years I knew a ton of them. He was a man who I learned much from. Not only about railroading but also about life!

I loved him dearly and was honored to be a pall barer at his funeral when he passed away in August of 1972.

John Cardamone taught me well in the crew dispatchers office, back during the summers of 1960 and 1961. This was one thankless job to be sure, but an interesting one at the same time.

John and I have remained close friends for over fifty four years. My first day on the clerks roster was the first day that I actually worked for pay, which was February 18, 1960.

Every railroader remembers their roster date. It's called their seniority date. This governs where they stand, when it comes to bidding for jobs.

There were seven pages of seniority dates for over 500 clerks from Hornell to Pt. Jervis, N.Y. I was so new, I had to write my name in at the bottom of the last page.

Retiring thirty seven years later, I was number nine on the whole roster.

Of course many of the jobs on the early roster were now long gone!

The pay in 1960 for a clerk was a daily rate of $18.40 or $92.00 per week.

When I took an early retirement thirty-seven years later in 1997, I was earning $50,000 a year as a Manager in the Crew Dispatching Office of Conrail in Dearborn, Michigan.

The best part about the railroad for me though, was the love of the job that I had. There never was one day, that I dreaded going to work.

There might have been somthing I would rather be doing, but never because I hated my job or disliked any of the people I worked with. Never, ever!

I could write a book about that great adventure alone.

Maybe someday I will.

The Erie Railroad and the Delaware, Lackawanna and Western Railroad merged in October of 1960 and became known as the Erie Lackawanna. The Lackawanna main tracks from Buffalo to Binghamton N.Y. for the main part were mostly torn up. All of their business came over to the former Erie's rails. For a short while the combined roads turned a small profit, but things soon started to go bad for all the railroads in the Northeast.

There were many reasons for it: Too much regulation, a huge redundancy in trackage, way too much track maintence that was needed, but always deferred for a lack of funds. Probably the biggest reason of all though was the amount of rail freight that was lost to the trucking industry, because of the building of the Interstate Highway System, during the 1950's and 1960's!

For all these reasons along with many more, it sounded the death knell for the Northeast's major railroads; The Penn-Central, Erie Lackawanna, Reading, Lehigh Valley, Central of New Jersey and Lehigh Hudson River. Something new that helped the railroads during the early to mid 1960's, but hurt the employees bad, was the blocking of train consists, which practically eliminated the old way of switching cars of entire trains every 100 miles.

The main switching facility for the EL was Bison Yard in Buffalo, only 90 rail miles away from Hornell. Because of this small procedure, which ended up being big, Hornell was down from twenty one yard engines a day in 1960, to just three yard jobs a day in 1964 and down to only one by 1967!

All the major switching on the railroad was now being done either east or west of Hornell.

Although, Hornell had been pretty much eliminated as a switching point,

It still remained a large crew change point, which was a blessing for the city.

Its railroad location between the other terminals, made this an ideal spot!

The Pennsylvania-New York Central merger of February 1, 1968 became the largest corporate bankruptcy in history in 1970.

Erie Lackawanna passenger service from New York City to Chicago and Buffalo, started being eliminated in the Fall of 1967 and by early January of 1970, this service was entirely gone.

The last straw for the Erie Lackawanna was Hurricane Agnes in late June of 1972. Agnes stalled right over our area and dumped record rain on us over a five to seven day period! It wiped out large sections of trackage all the way along the line from Meadville, Pa. to New Jersey, forcing the EL finally into bankruptcy. During that period our yard office in Hornell was flooded out three times in just one week alone. A cemetery around Wilkes-Barre, Pa. was opened up by the storm and caskets were seen floating away down the flooded streets! The repercussions from this terrible storm were huge.

The Hornell, Corning, and Elmira area had many deaths and suffered much destruction! I, myself suffered no damage from the storm and felt so guilty for so much suffering of other people, I volunteered my service's to help clean out the yard office each time it flooded with General Yardmaster Charlie Sikso. The mud in some places was six inches thick. The two of us took twelve hours each time to get the job done. It was one filthy, job!

Because of all the damage to the Erie Lackawanna plant, we had to dead-head our crews by taxi all over the northeast to man our trains that had been diverted over other roads, that suffered little or no damage, such as we did!

Four years later on April 1st of 1976 the Erie Lackawanna, along with the five other major railroads in the north east, were all rolled into the huge federally funded railroad called Consolidated Rail Corporation or Conrail for short.

The Chicago to Boston and New York markets now had three main line railroads. The former Erie Lackawanna, the former Pennsylvania and the former New York Central all serving this same general area.

It took no stretch of the imagination at all to know, one of the three had to go.

That one would, of course be the EL, the one in the middle, and the smallest one by far of the big three.

Our traffic, and we had a ton of it at one time, would eventually be rerouted over the former New York Central and Pennsylvania main lines, thereby bypassing Hornell, almost entirely.

By 1982 almost all of the former Erie Lackawanna Railroad jobs had left Hornell and the few that were left would be gone in a short time thereafter.

Conrail may have been a huge blessing for the former Pennsylvania and New York Central Railroads, but for the Erie Lackawanna, and Hornell in particular, it was a complete train wreck, no pun intended!

At times railroads could be quite unreliable too!

The first dinette set we bought in 1964 was shipped from Wausau, Wisconsin by rail. It would take six to seven days to make the journey and be unloaded at the Hornell freight house. In the meantime, we would be eating off of TV trays. The boxcar with our shipment, got lost in transit and ended up in Shreveport, La. It was located four weeks later as a no-bill! A trip that should have taken no more than a week at most, took five weeks.

Hornell at one time had a big and thriving downtown. There was a Sears and Roebuck, J.C. Penneys, F.W. Woolworths five and dime, J.J. Newberrys five and dime, Tuttle and Rockwells Department Store, an Army and Navy Store, Jacks Sports Shop, three mens clothing stores, three fine ladies stores, along with six shoe stores, and three jewelry stores.

Three drug stores with lunch counters. There once were four movie theatres along with three nice restaurants. Ted Mikes and Koskies, both newspaper and magazine stores. Also Koskies record and TV store.

There were 28 mom and pop grocery stores that were scattered all over the city. There was a delishous homemade ice cream shop called Matties.

All of the above mentioned are now gone. In fact, most have been gone for many years.

There were a ton of gin mills. Only a few remain today.

Where there were twelve main churches, there are only six left today.

Hornell High sports teams were once rated AA for high school sports but are now rated only B, on account of the decline in the male population in grades nine thru twelve.

Hornell was an excellent place to raise a family and most important, it was a better then average place when growing up as a teenager!

Today there is a force of about 400 employees that work in the former diesel shops of the Erie-Lackawanna, now repairing subway cars, but that's about it. There are no yard switch engines any more, sitting at East Ave crossing, waiting to go to work. Where the tracks of the yards once were, there is now one big empty field, all over grown with large trees and weeds.

It is so sad and down heartening to know of what once was and now is no more. One Truly Sad Connection.............

As a note of interest, are two unique stories of railroading and myself.

In addition to being a career railroad employee, I am also a big railroad fan as you can probably tell. Especially when it comes to my railroads, first the Erie, then the Erie Lackawanna and finally Conrail. I collect all kinds of railroad books and buy most of the books from a place called Rons Books in Harrison, N.Y.

Last year (2013) I purchased a book called Erie Railroad Facilities in New York State. In the book on page 70, there is a picture of a woman with a small boy of about ten waiting to go on a railroad excursion from

Corning, N.Y. to Letchworth State Park at Portageville, N.Y., some seventy odd miles west of Corning. The date on the picture is Sunday, June 11, 1950.

After looking at the picture a couple of times, and finally with the aid of a magnifying glass, the picture is of my stepmother and me. I remember going on that trip with her and my father, who was working the trip as a trainman.

How unique is it to look backward in time, in a book and see yourself at the age of ten, when you are now seventy-three.

The odds would be enormous, maybe even gargantuan, I would bet.

One More Unbelievable Connection.............

The second story is more of a human interest one, but still a railroad one as well. I once held a midnight to eight, yard clerks job in the Hornell eastbound yard office during 1965-66. The first thing I had to do when coming on duty, was to call Elmira Yard and give the clerk there certain reports from our office.

The clerk in Elmira, would in turn give some reports back to me that I would record in a ledger. The clerk in Elmira was a real nice guy by the name of Joe Barrett. After a short while we became friendly with each other and would talk about the railroad, families, sports, politics, etc.

He was married with a two year old daughter and I was married with a two year old son.

One Summer, Sunday in 1968, we took Michael who was now five to Eldridge Amusement Park in Elmira, N.Y., for the day.

In late afternoon, on the way home we stopped at a Red Barn burger joint, in west Elmira. Sitting right behind me with our backs to each other in a booth was a man, his wife and daughter, who I thought was about five years old.

Although I had never seen these people before, the man's voice sure sounded familiar to me. If we had been facing each other, I probably wouldn't have even picked up on it, but sitting as we were, I sure did!

One Sweet Connection coming up!...............

Although Joe and I hadn't had any Connection with each other in over two years, I recognized the voice as being his. At least I thought it was his voice, anyways.

One way or another, I was determined to find out for sure!

I turned and spoke. "Hey Joe, how about passing me your ketchup, will you please?" "Sure thing!" came his reply. Jean asked me if I knew who this guy was? "I think so, but I'm not absolutely positive." "What do you mean, you think so?" "Hey Joe, how about passing me some salt, would you please?" "Did you call me Joe?" "Yeah, that's your name isn't it?"

"Yes, but how did you know ?" I had him now!

"We work together on the Erie Lackawanna and now when you get out in public, you don't even know who I am." "No, I don't know who you are and I never worked with you on the railroad either." "Sure you did back in 1965 and 1966!"

"We talked on the phone five nights a week and now you don't even know who I am." By now Jeans face was fire engine red from embarrassment.

"Oh my God, are you Pete from Hornell?" "That's me pal!" With that we both jumped up out of our seats and gave each other one big hug.

We moved into their booth with them and caught up with each other.

Joe was now the Claim Agent for the railroad in the Elmira area.

It was a great ending to a perfect day.

A Renewed Connection!..................

As it so happened, Joe was a brother-in-law to a railroad engineer friend of mine, Rick Larnerd, from the Scranton, Pa. area. What a small world, my thoughts.

The Connections Seem To Go On, And On, And On, And!…...…………..

A FUTURE DENTIST

Bill Pearson graduated from Hornell High school a year ahead of me and was in college studying to eventually becoming a dentist. At the time of this story, he was home from college for the summer recess.

His father Don who I called for work many times, was a yard switchman in the Hornell yards of the Erie Railroad.

One early evening, in July of 1960, around 7:00pm, Bill, Jerry Hancock, Jim Logan and I were sitting at the bar, in the Ponce De Leon Restaurant in Hornell having a beer and talking over what we might do for entertainment for the night. Someone piped up, "Lets go over to Lake Demons."

"What's over there?" "Well, there's a Girl Scout camp and where there's Girl Scouts, there's bound to be female councilors about our age."

With this last statement, no further discussion was needed.

I volunteered to drive and left to go and get my car which was parked two short blocks away. "I'll be back and pick you guys up right out front in about five minutes."

I pulled up in front of the Ponce and honked the horn for the three of them to come out. Only Jerry and Jim, came out. "Where's Bill, in the john?" " No he's not going." "What do you mean he's not going?"

"He's changed his mind, he doesn't want to go." "Baloney on that."

"He probably thinks with him along, we won't have enough room."

"Well, he's mistaken, because we'll make room if need be!"

Fortunately, a car pulled out of a parking space just ahead of me, so I pulled right in his now vacated spot.

"I'm going in and get Bill, you guys wait out here." "We'll be right out."

There he sat, with a big smile on his face, waving me away. "I really don't want to go Pete, and besides you only have room for six people in your car, not eight." "It would never work out." "Its better this way, just the three of you go and have a good time without me."

I realized right away that Bill was doing this more for our sake then really not wanting to go and I wasn't going to have any part of it!

"Bill, we'll make room, even if a couple of the girls have to sit on someone's lap." "Besides, theres no guarantee that we'll meet up with any girls!"

"Look Bill, if you don't go, I'm not going, its as simple as that."

"And, I'm gonna sit right here until you change your mind, even if it takes all night." He just laughed in response to my pleading, but by now, he knew he had a tiger by the tail. A tiger that wasn't about to let go!

"Then it will take all night Pete, because I'm not going, and that's it, end of story!" We'll see about that brother, my thoughts.

After a few more minutes of back and forth banter between the two of us, Jerry came back in. "Are we going or not, we've been sitting out front, waiting in the car, for almost twenty minutes now."

"We're working on it," came my reply. Finally, Bill looked at me and spoke up and It was like music to my ears!

"Alright Pete, I'll go." "You have talked me into it."

"Not because I really want to go, but only because I don't want to spoil things for you guys." "Whatever your reason Bill, lets go."

Don't you just love the power of perseverance and determination! Nothing like it in the world! At Lake Demons, we met up with four nice young ladies, all about our age and the eight of us piled into my Pontiac Catalina and drove to Molly's Diner in Bath, N.Y., a short distance away for burgers, fries and cokes. By the way, Molly's would be a landing spot for two hungry teenagers and I, ten years further down the road. Another connection yet, I now have a grandaughter named Molly! Are you ready for this?

Bill Pearson, my friend who didn't want to go and whose mind I finally changed, ended up meeting a young lady from Pittsburg, Pa. that night, who would end up being his FUTURE WIFE and the MOTHER of his children.

If not for my timely perseverance in prodding him to go, their meeting would never have taken place. Not in a million years.

You can't make this stuff up!!

Way more better then fiction, don't you think?

Just one more important thing on earth, I guess I had to take care of!

This one even before my encounter with the Angel from Heaven, which was now just two short months away.

Was this test of my determination and tenacity, an audition for all the important things that still lay ahead?

One   Heaven   Sent   And   Received Connection!............................

As a footnote, Bill would go on to become a respected dentist in Hornell!

DR. JAMES R. KELLY-PART I

My Doctor was Dr. James R. Kelly, a GP/Surgeon who was a very respected Doctor in Hornell. His father Raymond, was also a GP and Surgeon. His brother John was a Gynecologist and Obstetrician.

Dr. Raymond was now in retirement, but still gave physicals for the Erie Railroad.

My appendix or that general area where it was located, had been bothering me for some time now, but the pain or discomfort would always come and go and never seemed to last for more than a few minutes.

Sometimes it felt like I had a catch there, but nothing serious, my thoughts.

I've been told It's a hard thing to pinpoint unless you have a real bad appendix attack or a ruptured appendix. X-rays and blood workup usually help doctors diagnose this illness that sometimes can prove fatal if not taken care of in an appropriate time and manner!

Today, an MRI enhancement can pinpoint the problem immediately!

Back in 1960 I'm sorry to say, there was no such thing as an MRI!

I had a full blown appendix attack in the early morning hours of September 20,1960, while I was at work as the third trick crew caller/messenger for the Erie Railroad.

I had called a crew at the Hornell YMCA for HB91, a Hoboken N.J. to Buffalo freight at 1:00am for an on duty reporting time of 3:00am.

On my way out of the Y, I bought some peanut butter crackers and a coke to munch on.

When I went back to pick the crew up at 1:30am to take them to an all night diner for breakfast, I had the worst cramps and pain in my lower abdomen and stomach, that I had ever suffered. It was all across me and made me want to bend right over, the pain was that great. Somehow I was able to finish my tour of duty and went home thinking if I could only get some rest, I would feel much better. I also thought maybe those peanut butter crackers were spoiled or something. Or maybe I had a stomach virus. Anything but my appendix, came to mind!

Sleep however, would not come. Only this horrible pain, which had me doubled over, even while curled up in a fetal position in bed.

My Grandmother Ward called Dr. James Kelly's office and got me an appointment for 12:30pm. When Dr. Kelly examined me, the pain had greatly diminished and was just about gone. The appendix had probably ruptured by now but Dr. Kelly's assessment of the situation was that I had a stomach virus. I could go to the hospital for tests, if I wanted to, just to be sure, but he didn't think that was really necessary at this time.

Not wanting to go to the hospital, I agreed with his opinion.

I went to my mom's place which was just across the street and got a little sleep off and on but woke up in the early evening with the worst pains yet that kept coming and going. It was just an unbelievable pain!

I hated to do it, but I had to mark off from work around 9:00pm for midnight. There was no way I could make it to work, not in my condition.

Sometime around 2:30am, on September 21st, when I tried to urinate, I was unable to do so, and I was in such terrible pain, that my mother called Dr. Kelly right up..

He advised her to take me to the St. James Hospital right away and he would meet us down there. Since she didn't have a car or even drive herself, she took me to the hospital in a taxi and they admitted me right away.

A catheter was inserted in me that allowed me to finally void. The urine was on the green side. Not Good!

Sometime around 5:00am I started vomiting up this dark green bile(poison) that had flooded my stomach area by now. Around seven o'clock an x-ray technician, Yvone, a schoolmate chum of mine and a cheerleader in my big game, came to get me in a wheel chair for X-rays. I was in bad shape by then and getting worse. I couldn't keep from bending over in the wheel chair, or pulling my legs up, since I was in such horrific pain. I tried to apologize to Yvonne, but I think she understood. Hopefully she did, anyways. If not, Yvonne, I'm sorry!

After the X-rays and blood work were finished, a nun came into my room with two long rubber hoses.

"What are you going to do with these things Sister?"

"I'm going to insert them into your stomach Peter by threading them through your nose and eventually down into your stomach." "They are going to help drain your stomach of this terrible poison, you're now experiencing."

"I don't think so Sister." "I know so Peter, so just lie back, and try to relax.

"You swallow each time I push and it will be just that much easier for you, ok?" She preceded to do her job and it went a lot easier than I ever thought it would!

To complicate matters even worse for me, Dr. Kelly fell back asleep after my mom called him and he didn't show up at the hospital until much later on, sometime later that morning.

After the blood work and X-ray's showed what my problem was, he operated on me sometime around 10:30am. By then I was a complete mess. My operating room nurse, told me later that they took TWO CUPS of peritonitis(poison) out of my stomach cavity area.

Dr. Kelly told me five months later that he did the best he could for me at the time, but in his mind there was no way I was going to survive this terrible disaster. I was just too far gone.

There was just too much poison through out my system and there was no way my body would be able to fight it all off. Or so he thought anyways!

It was just way too much to ask of anyone in this horrible condition.

I was going to be a goner for sure or so it seemed to him.

After the initial operation, Dr. Kelly told my mom and grandmothers that it was going to be nip and tuck and that he gave me a fifty-fifty chance of pulling through it. "What was I going to tell them, that you were in all probability going to die." "I felt that I had to give them some kind of hope even if there was very little hope to go on!" My mom said he told them I had a good heart and that I seemed to be a fighter so we'll just have to wait and see.The next twenty four hours would be most critical!

Five months later Dr. Kelly would tell me that he didn't give me the chance of a plugged nickel of pulling through. He said it was a huge miracle alone that I survived the first operation, let alone all the many complications to my system that came along afterwards.

I don't know why Dr. Kelly didn't put the drains in me at the end of the first operation since it was possible it could have saved me from having a second operation and the need to insert the drains at that time.

Maybe he thought he had gotten all or most of the peritonitis out of me. Maybe he thought it wasn't going to matter anyways. Or maybe a little bit of both. He never told me and I never asked. Just a thought though.

When the drains finally came out, the second incision was never stitched up. The wound site was left to heal from the inside out.

This was done just in case of another abscess forming. If and when it broke it would have an opening to drain from.

Just so the bad luck of 1960 never ceased coming; within five days of my release from the hospital, my temperature shot up to 103 degrees.

Dr. Kelly ordered an antibiotic. I never forgot the name of the drug.It was Chloramysetin. Each pill cost seventy five cents, which was a lot of money back in 1960. They did their job though as the newly formed abscess broke and drained out through the incision site.

Another terrible ordeal to go through, for sure!.

The second incision site would continue to drain blood and pus until it fully healed and finally closed up some six months later in late March of 1961!

It might have closed up a little sooner but a certain incident in mid February happened, which would greatly interfere with its healing!

Between my stubbornness in not going to the hospital a day earlier, to be completely checked out and Dr. Kelly falling back to sleep, I almost bought the farm, as the saying goes.

It didn't much matter anyways, in the late afternoon of the first operation. There was going to be a miraculous and divine intervention in all of this pain and suffering. It was now enroute and it was coming on the wings of four Angels. They were coming to get me and take me (my soul) away with them!

A Miraculous Angel/Human Connection was Now Underway!.........

Soul Escape

Sometime in the dark of the late afternoon of my first operation, when I was all alone and the anesthesia from the operation, had fully worn off, I suddenly became aware that something either spiritually, physically or maybe both was about to happen to me. Was I going to die or what? I don't think so! It was so eerie, but some kind of absolute calm had suddenly now come over me.

It is so hard to describe, even to this day.

My entire hospital room had now become bathed in a warm golden glow of light, and yet no lights in my room had been turned on.

How could that possibly be, were my thoughts. The majority of the soft light seemed to be coming from the window area. As if something had penetrated the closed window. Some kind of a warm soft light!

I suddenly sensed there was a small group of someone in my room right now, but I couldn't quite make them out. There was a sound of whispering and flapping! They seemed to be huddled all around me, sort of caring for me while at the same time, I was being bathed in this warm golden glow of light!

There was now a feeling of pure ecstasy, like nothing I had ever experienced before or since. It was like someone was holding me in the open cupped palms of their two hands. They were so big, so comforting and yet I was so small, but so secure at the same time.

There was absolutely nothing to fear!

In fact fear as an emotion, no longer even existed.

A Gathering Of Angels Now Connected With Me!...........

Such peacefulness as this feeling was, is so hard to adequately describe, even to this day!

You might say that it was an unconditional trust and love of the highest order. What a wonderful and glorious feeling, my thoughts!

I sensed that something, much more bigger than I was about to occur.

I remember there was a definite scent of incense in the air too.

Where did that wonderful smell come from, my thoughts.

The Connection with everything all together was simply awesome!

I didn't quite know what was going to take place but I knew that I didn't want to fight it, what ever it was. Just totally accept it and bask in its warm, glowing light.Whatever was about to happen to me, I knew it was going to be something quite special and wonderful. I had never felt quite so alive!

It was like perfection in reality! The whole journey would end up being one wonderful and unbelievable experience.

An Angel/Human Connection Was About To Take Wing!..........

Suddenly, ever so slowly now, my soul lifted upwards, rising up away from my body and remained there, somewhat suspended over it. It was a complete uncoupling of my soul away from my body! Is this what its like to die, my thoughts.

Am I dead or alive, not being quite sure of either?

What is taking place here? Where am I going? My body hasn't moved at all, but what must be my soul is just floating in mid air, and is barely moving, just slowly floating or hovering over my body and swaying back and forth, like in a slight breeze. One comfortable feeling!

My body lying right beneath me now, with its eyes half open, half closed, looks so cold and foreign. Just a mere shell now, nothing more.

Maybe I am dead or at least my body is! I seem to be so alive and yet my body below me is so motionless. I floated there for a short time and then my soul started to move, ever so slowly, away from the bed where my body lay.

It was a complete trust that you were in the realm of someone or something, that was so much bigger than yourself, but very secure at the same time. What an exquisite and wonderful feeling this was!

Maybe it was the almighty and that he was going to take care of me, not only for now, but for all eternity. It was the most beautiful feeling of serenity and love that anyone could ever wish to experience. Total unconditional LOVE!

That was the best way to describe it. Talk about a comfort zone, this was it!

Almost immediately now, I found myself in what I would call a funnel. To me it was a funnel because I was going upwards, like in a large tube and at the same time, I was going around slowly, in a counter-clockwise motion. I could now see clearly the four Angels, that must have been in my hospital room with me!

They were all around me now. They seemed to be supporting and guiding me upwards, ever upwards and singing out the most beautiful music. It was some kind of music that I had never heard before, and it was so hauntingly beautiful.

And boy, could those Angels ever sing it out!

As we were slowly going around, we were also floating upward, like in a swimming motion, and the feeling was one of complete tranquility.

At the same time I was also bathed in beautiful sun light, just like the soft light in my hospital room and yet there was no sun. Quite surreal, my thoughts!.........

The Angels all wore transparent see through gowns with nothing to see except thin air. Their gowns were of sheer silk, in light pastel colors of blue, pink, yellow, and green. They seemed to shimmer and rotate all around as they continued in guiding me ever upwards!.

What held my attention the most though, was this wonderful music that the Angels were singing. It was the most wonderful music this side of Heaven,(no pun intended) I thought. What kind of music is this anyways?

I had never heard it before and it seemed like the Angels were singing it especially for me or maybe singing it to me.

I had always loved music, all kinds of music, but I had never heard anything so beautiful and uplifting, in all my life, as was this melodious, angelic music.......

Now it seemed as if the Angels were shouting out this music to me.

I would never hear such beautiful music like this again for over a decade, sometime in the 1970's. That's when this Angelic New Age music would finally come on the scene, to uplift one's spirits.

They say that music is the heart of the soul.

A truer statement then that has never been uttered!

Whenever I am asked today, what kind of music I heard on this special day, I would have to answer, Angelic New Age. I or no one else for that matter, had ever heard of this kind of music back in 1960! Think about this piece of important information. One very important point to ponder here!

How was it possible that I could hear such beautiful music as this, music that had not yet been introduced, and wouldn't be for over a decade or more later? What a sneak preview this was!

An Angelic Music/Me Connection!.............................

Almost immediately now, the Angels and the funnel were gone and I now found myself all alone in a long dark tunnel. I was accelerating in this tunnel at an alarmingly high rate of speed toward the far end.

As fast as I was flying toward the end of the tunnel, there was nothing to fear or worry about, just total security and a complete feeling of peacefulness.

At the far end of the tunnel was a bright light. It was the brightest light I had ever seen, way far brighter than the sun itself, and yet it wasn't blinding at all! So surreal, my thoughts.

The nearer I got to the light, the brighter it got, until when I was almost at the end, it slowly, ever so slowly started to burn away or contract, and was completely gone by the time I had reached the end of the tunnel.

At the far end of the tunnel where the bright light had once been, now stood a man in a full length robe, holding an oaken staff in his right hand.

He was all dressed in white, including his sandals. He had shoulder length white hair and a fully trimmed white beard.

I wondered, if this might be the Lord himself, or maybe St. Peter. He was certainly one handsome man, whoever he was.

He was smiling at me as if he had known me forever. And maybe, just maybe, he had, my thoughts. If I had to choose who this was, I would say Jesus!

To my right and to his left was a huge oaken door. This man, whoever he was, did not speak to me, but just nodded his head towards the big door.

I sensed that everything was ok and that he now wanted me to open and go through the door into wherever!

So very slowly, I opened the door and went into the most beautiful place I had ever seen in all my life.

Believe me, trying to describe it adequately is beyond human ability to give it true justice, but I'll surely try!

It was forever daylight there, and yet there was no sun!

Of course there was no night.

Everything seemed to be in Technicolor, but the colors were so much more vivid and brilliant then colors back on earth.

The sky was the bluest blue, with not a cloud in sight.

The grass was so green and well manicured.

All the buildings were of very thick, solid, and transparent gold.

The roads were litterly paved with gold!

There was a huge golden fortress in the middle that stood about 45 to 50 feet high. It ran off to my left, into the distance, as far as the eye could see, and it seemed like here, one could see forever!

There was a huge gate in the middle of the fortress.

One could sense that there was no pain or suffering here!

So this is what Heaven looks and feels like, I thought.

Truly Amazing!

What a beautiful place, so peaceful, and tranquil.

This was one place d, in which you always wanted to reach, but once there, you never wanted to leave. Thats the feeling I got anyways!

One beautiful, and unbelievable place at the same time!

A Wondrous Heavenly Connection...........

In the time I was in Heaven, I never saw anyone else. No one, except the four wonderful Angels that accompanied me from my room, to being with me in the funnel, along with the handsome man at the far end of the tunnel, all dressed in white. There were only a few people that I knew at the time, that had passed on, that I could have seen there anyways. I might have seen my two grandfathers, Ruth's grandfather or aunt. but I didn't see anyone while I was there.

I wasn't aware of how long I was in Heaven, but time there didn't matter anyways.

Suddenly, without any warning, my soul departed and was gone from Heaven in a flash.

As soothing and uplifting as new age music is today, the Angels music was so much better than even the new age music of today!

This wonderful music didn't come along until sometime in the 1970's and yet I heard this special kind of wonderful music, way back in 1960!!! Incredible!

Remember, ALL Things are Possible with God................

Many years later, one afternoon in 1977 or 1978, I picked up the Bible at home and not knowing quite why, was drawn to the last book in the New Testamint called the Book of Revelations. It was a book in the Bible that I had never looked at before. There I read of the description of Heaven, and WOW!

My thoughts were; hey, I've seen that movie before. Been there, done that! It was so awesome and surreal that It raised goose bumps all over my arms, neck and back.

Still A Heavenly Connection, Many Years Later!...........................

To hear wonderful music like I heard on that day in 1960 go to amazon.com music. listen to or purchase Michele Ippolitos, Celestial voices. Clair Marlos Angel is an other wonderful angelic piece as is, Erik Berglands Angel Healing, which lasts for 52 minutes.

Remember all this beautiful music did not come on the scene until sometime in the 1970s or later and yet I heard music like this, in September of 1960! Totally amazing!

Picture of me and my stepmother at the Corning,
N.Y. station on June 10,1950. Courtesy of Preston
Johnson and Morning Sun Books Inc.

HORNELL JAYVEE CAGERS—Coach Bud O'Neil of the Hornell High School Junior Varsity checks a play with three members of his squad—Jerry Prior, Capt. Sal Fiscina and Pete Babcock (left to right). The Hornell Jayvees have won 11 straight since loss of their opener.

Hornell Jayvees Win 11
Since Opening Defeat

The performance has been sort of overlooked inasmuch as all jayvee teams play in the shadow of the varsity, but right now Bud O'Neil's Hornell High School Junior Varsity cagers have an 11-game winning streak on the first.

Back in their very first game of the season the HHS Jayvees lost by four points at Painted Post 40-56. That is the only game the Hor-nell youngsters have lost. They've copped 11 in a row including a close two-pointer over the Wellsville Jayvees.

Naturally, one of the main purposes of any JV team is to develop youngsters who can take over varsity assignments in future years. On the HHS squad, Eric Shultz, Jim Flaitz and Bill Crowe have been handling the "inside" job around the boards.

Pete Babcock and Jerry Prior lead the scoring for the team at 187 and 151. Shultz is the big man on the squad at 6-3. Flaitz is 6-1.

Hornell JV Record

26	Painted Post	40
50	Olean	30
54	Perlew	33
49	Olean	37
51	Wellsville	43
56	Batavia	43
61	BoD	32
54	Batavia	37
46	CNS	47
55	Painted Post	51
69	Aquinas	48

Individual Scoring

	G	F	T
Pete Babcock	60	37	157
Jerry Prior	60	31	151
Sal Fiscina	32	28	92
Bill Crowe	23	15	61
Eric Shultz	32	8	50
Jim Flaitz	21	5	47
John McGrAsh	16	12	44
Arden Page	8	1	13
George Cottrell	4	1	9
George Comfort	2	4	8
W. Connors	2	0	8
R. Babcock	3	0	8

Hornell Jayvees win 11 straight article was taken sometime in late January of 1957. Courtesy of Hornell Evening Tribune.

My Senior Picture. Courtesy James Grimm &
Memory Studio Hornell, NY was taken in August of 1957.

HORNELL, N. Y., SATURDAY, MARCH 1, 1958

Petie 1 Short of Record; HHS Wins, 96-72

Petie Babcock Scoring Giant
At 112 Lbs.... Hits 36 Points

It was "Petie Babcock Night" at the Hornell High School basketball hall last evening.

The little man — who has to jump on the scales neat hard to make them read 112 pounds and in HHS uniform at 5 feet, 4 inches — put on a tremendous 36-point scoring display as the Red Raiders closed out their season with a 96-72 win over St. Anthony of Padua of Watkins Glen.

This was Petie's Party practically all the way. He was one of five seniors Coach Ollie Hartman started and he hit two quick baskets in the opening minutes. He had 16 points at halftime.

Hartman brought him to the bench in the second half. Then when the HHS attack started to bog down and Padua came up within 9 points, "Petie" came back in the lineup. Quickly he rang the bell three times and Hornell was

off to the races again.

Going into the last 4 minutes, no one was hardly looking at the scoreboard. Everyone was counting Babcock's total. When it became apparent that he actually had a shot at the school's all-time scoring record his teammates started to feed "Petie".

Four times he had free throws and four times he scored as the crowd roared . . . he hit 'em from the corners and from out front . . .

and at the finish he was one point shy of the school record.

But the Raiders made sure he "broke" the standard just for kicks . . . As the buzzer sounded the Raiders swept the little man to their shoulders and carried him to one basket and from atop the massed shoulders he flunked the shot that "gave him 36."

Babcock poured in 18 points in the last quarter alone . . . he was 16 for 33 from the field (a shooting percentage of 48 per cent) and 4-for-4 at the foul line.

The likeable little kid was both breathless and speechless when it was over. He's a youngster who has seldom missed a practice and cheered for the club from the bench many nights. Now he has an occasion to remember as he bowed out of scholastic competition.

The game was a free-scorer as the 168-point total for the two clubs would indicate. It's the highest score for the two clubs since 1945-56 when the Raiders hit 92 points against Corning Northside.

Hornell was in front on baskets by Babcock and Stook after an opening foul by Padua. Then the Raiders pulled away 28-20 at the quarter and 49-28 at halftime. As the game moved Padua cut Hornell's lead to 9 in the second half. Then Petie set off the fireworks again and the scoreboard just managed to contain the final figures.

Notes: The crowd was there to cheer for Babcock and once the students started to chant "We Want Babcock" when the little man was on the bench . . . Hornell ended its season with a very

Petie Babcock . . . big scoring display in a small package.

fine 12-6 record . . . Dave Guenther, Al Stook, Jerry Prior and Bob Egan other seniors who closed out last night . . . the Raiders held a "shower party" later to celebrate the windup of the campaign

Hornell

	SA	FG	FT	F	T
Babcock	33	16	4	4	36
Guenther	12	5	0	4	10
Stook		6	1	3	13
Prior		4	1	1	9
Smith		2	0	1	4
Egan		1	0	4	2
Sartino		1	1	1	3
Padua		1	0	0	2
Cantolo		2	1	1	5
Total	108	38	13	8	96

Padua

	SA	FG	FT	F	T
Nawotski		6	3	2	15
Volpe		8	2	5	18
Nagara		5	4	1	14
Nicosia		4	1	4	9
Nowaski		2	1	1	5
Total	38	29	22	14	72
Hornell		28	49	86—96
Padua		20	28	55—72

Basketball stories. Courtesy Hornell Evening
Tribune. Circa March 1, 1958.

ST. JAMES MERCY HOSPITAL
HORNELL, NEW YORK

Room __324 semi__ Case No. ____
Ward ____
Rate __$17__

Name __Babcock, Peter__ Address __23 Elm St., Hornell, N. Y.__
Bill to __Self__ Address ____

MEMO		DATE	EXPLANATION		AMT. CHARGED	AMT. CREDITED	BALANCE DUE	Room No.
	1	SEP20-60	PRIV.ROOM		* 17.00		* 17.00	D 324-
	2	SEP21-60	PRIV.ROOM		* 17.00			D * -
	3	SEP21-60	OPER.ROOM		* 30.00			D * -
	4	SEP21-60	AN'STHESIA		* 10.00			D * -
	5	SEP21-60	X-RAY		* 15.00			D * -
	6	SEP21-60		GL.&SUPPLY	* 5.00			D * -
	7	SEP21-60	SP.DRUGS		* 25.85		* 119.85	D * -
	8	SEP22-60	PRIV.ROOM		* 17.00			D * -
	9	SEP22-60	SP.DRUGS		* 14.90		* 151.75	D * 3-
	10	SEP23-60	PRIV.ROOM		* 20.00			D 327-
	11	SEP23-60	SP.DRUGS		* 9.30			D * -
	12	SEP23-60	X-RAY		* 15.00		* 196.05	D * -
	13	SEP24-60	PRIV.ROOM		* 20.00			D * -
	14	SEP24-60	SP.DRUGS		* 16.25		* 232.30	D * -
	15	SEP25-60	PRIV.ROOM		* 20.00			D * -
	16	SEP25-60	SP.DRUGS		* 1.00		* 253.30	D * -
	17	SEP26-60	PRIV.ROOM		* 20.00			D * -
	18	SEP26-60	SP.DRUGS		* 22.60		* 295.90	D * -
	19	SEP27-60	PRIV.ROOM		* 20.00			D * -
	20	SEP27-60	SP.DRUGS		* 9.60		* 325.50	D * -
	21	SEP28-60	PRIV.ROOM		* 20.00			D * -
	22	SEP28-60	X-RAY		* 10.00		* 363.00	D * -
	23	SEP28-60	SP.DRUGS		*		* 383.00	D * -
	24	SEP29-60	PRIV.ROOM		* 20.00			D * -

The Red Cross Supplies Blood Without
Any Charge. Any Transfusion Fee
is for Administration Only.

F.R.00-77221-1052-10H

CODED CHARGES
A-NURSERY E-TELEPHONE X-THERAPY
B-EMERGENCY ROOM F-TRANSFUSION W-OXYGEN
C-METABOLISM G-CIRCUMCISION
D-E.K.G. H-E.K.G. READING

X-Ray Charges
Include the professional services
of Drs. MacFerland and Auringer
Laboratory Charges
NOT included in this bill

ST. JAMES MERCY HOSPITAL
HORNELL, NEW YORK

Room ____ Case No. ____
Ward ____
Rate ____

Name __Babcock, Peter__ Address ____
Bill to ____ Address ____

MEMO		DATE	EXPLANATION		AMT. CHARGED	AMT. CREDITED	BALANCE DUE	Room No.
	1						* 383.00	
	2	SEP29-60	SP.DRUGS		* 2.10		* 385.10	D * -
	3	SEP30-60	PRIV.ROOM		* 20.00			D * -
	4	SEP30-60		MISC.CHGE	* 5.00			D * F
	5	SEP30-60	SP.DRUGS		* 4.80		* 414.90	D * -
	6	OCT-1-60	PRIV.ROOM		* 20.00			D * -
	7	OCT-1-60	SP.DRUGS		* 22.70			D * -
	8	OCT-1-60	OPER.ROOM		* 20.00			D * -
	9	OCT-1-60	AN'STHESIA		* 10.00		* 487.60	D * -
	10	OCT-2-60	PRIV.ROOM		* 20.00		* 507.60	D * -
	11	OCT-3-60	PRIV.ROOM		* 20.00		* 527.60	D * -
	12	OCT-4-60	PRIV.ROOM		* 20.00			D * -
	13	OCT-4-60		DRESSINGS	* 7.80			D * -
	14	OCT-4-60	SP.DRUGS		* 7.30		* 562.70	D * -
	15	OCT-5-60	PRIV.ROOM		* 20.00			D * -
	16	OCT-5-60	SP.DRUGS		* 4.00		* 586.70	D * -
	17	OCT-6-60	PRIV.ROOM		* 20.00			D * -
	18	OCT-6-60	X-RAY		* 20.00			D * -
	19	OCT-6-60	SP.DRUGS		* 23.15		* 649.85	D * -
	20	OCT-7-60	PRIV.ROOM		* 20.00			D * -
	21	OCT-7-60	SP.DRUGS		* 13.75		* 683.60	D * -
	22	OCT-8-60	PRIV.ROOM		* 20.00			D * -
	23	OCT-8-60	SP.DRUGS		* 39.20			D * -
	24	OCT-8-60		MISC.CHGE	* 5.00		* 747.80	D * F

The Red Cross Supplies Blood Without
Any Charge. Any Transfusion Fee
is for Administration Only.

F.R.00-77221-1052-10H

CODED CHARGES
A-NURSERY E-TELEPHONE K-THERAPY
B-EMERGENCY ROOM F-TRANSFUSION W-OXYGEN
C-METABOLISM G-CIRCUMCISION
D-E.K.G. H-E.K.G. READING

X-Ray Charges
Include the professional services
of Drs. MacFerland and Auringer
Laboratory Charges
NOT included in this bill

Bill from Saint James Hospital for ruptured appendix from
September 20, 1960 through October 20 of 1960.

ST. JAMES MERCY HOSPITAL
HORNELL, NEW YORK

Room............... Case No.............
Ward...............
Rate...............

Name Babcock, Peter...Address...........................

Bill to...Address...........................

MEMO		DATE	EXPLANATION	AMT. CHARGED	AMT. CREDITED	BALANCE DUE	ROOM No.
	1	OCT-6-60	DRESSINGS	★ 1.10		★ 749.50	D ● --
	2	OCT-9-60	PRIV.ROOM	★ 20.00		★ 769.50	D ● --
	3	OCT10-60	SP.DRUGS	★ 2.75			D ● --
	4	OCT10-60	X-RAY	★ 10.00		★ 782.25	D ● --
	5	OCT11-60	PRIV.ROOM	★ 20.00			D ● --
	6	OCT11-60	SP.DRUGS	★ 1.55		★ 803.80	D ● --
	7	OCT12-60	PRIV.ROOM	★ 20.00			D ● --
	8	OCT12-60	SP.DRUGS	★ 4.35		★ 828.15	D ● --
	9	OCT13-60	PRIV.ROOM	★ 20.00			D ● --
	10	OCT13-60	SP.DRUGS	★ 15.75		★ 863.90	D ● --
	11	OCT14-60	PRIV.ROOM	★ 20.00			D ● --
	12	OCT14-60	X-RAY	★ 10.00		★ 893.90	D ● --
	13	OCT14-60	SP.DRUGS	★ 9.05		★ 902.95	D ● --
	14	OCT15-60	PRIV.ROOM	★ 20.00		★ 922.95	D ● --
	15	OCT16-60	PRIV.ROOM	★ 20.00			D ● --
	16	OCT16-60	SP.DRUGS	★ 3.85		★ 946.80	D ● --
	17	OCT17-60	PRIV.ROOM	★ 20.00			D ● --
	18	OCT17-60	SP.DRUGS	★ 9.00		★ 975.80	D ● --
	19	OCT18-60	PRIV.ROOM	★ 20.00			D ● --
	20	OCT18-60	SP.DRUGS	★ 4.95			D ● --
	21	OCT18-60	X-RAY	★ 15.00		1,015.75	D ● --
	22	OCT19-60	PRIV.ROOM	★ 20.00		1,045.95	D ● --
	23	OCT19-60	SP.DRUGS	★ 10.20		1,065.95	D ● --
	24	OCT20-60	PRIV.ROOM	★ 20.00			D ● --

The Red Cross Supplies Blood Without
Any Charge. Any Transfusion Fee
is for Administration Only.

P.B.CO.—68589-788-10M

------- CODED CHARGES -------
A—NURSERY   E—TELEPHONE
B—EMERGENCY ROOM   F—TRANSFUSION
C—METABOLISM   G—CIRCUMCISION
D—E.K.G.   H—E.K.G. READING

Laboratory Charges
NOT included in this bill

ST. JAMES MERCY HOSPITAL
HORNELL, NEW YORK

Room............... Case No.............
Ward...............
Rate...............

Name Babcock, Peter...Address...........................

Bill to...Address...........................

MEMO		DATE	EXPLANATION	AMT. CHARGED	AMT. CREDITED	BALANCE DUE	ROOM No.
	1					1,065.95	
	2	OCT20-60	MISC.CHGE	★ 6.00		1,071.95	D ● E
	3	OCT21-60	SP.DRUGS CORRECT'N		★ 6.90	1,065.05	D ● --
	4						
	5						
	6						
	7						
	8						
	9						
	10						
	11		Your claim has been sent in to Travelers including lab				
	12		fee, $83				
	13						
	14						
	15						
	16						
	17						
	18						
	19						
	20						
	21						
	22						
	23						
	24						

The Red Cross Supplies Blood Without
Any Charge. Any Transfusion Fee
is for Administration Only.

P.N.CO.—65X56-756-10M

------- CODED CHARGES -------
A—NURSERY   E—TELEPHONE
B—EMERGENCY ROOM   F—TRANSFUSION
C—METABOLISM   G—CIRCUMCISION
D—E.K.G.   H—E.K.G. READING

Laboratory Charges
NOT included in this bill

Hospital bill from Saint James Hospital
September 20th through October 20th, 1960, continued.

Return From Heaven

In one big flash, I was back from Heaven with a single Angel by my side.

We were in my room, in the hospital, at the top of the ceiling looking down at the body of a young male in the bed directly below us.

The young man had an IV in his right arm and two tubes running from his nose into a bottle with green liquid being drained from his stomach.

His eyes were half closed. It has to be me, I thought, but I wasn't 100% sure. Right next to me at the ceiling, just off to my left was the Angel.

We were about to have a conversation. It would not be a very long one, but it would be an awe inspiring one, just the same! It would not be of the talking variety, but of a much faster thought process.

So much faster then any communication on earth that was possible at that time or even is to this day.

I thought, he thought, so on, so forth. It was going to be at warp speed.... I'm going to put it into words, but none the less, it was a thought to thought process.

First of all, I needed confirmation that the body below us was mine, so I spoke (thought) up.

"Is that me, lying in the bed down there right below us?"

"Yes, that's you." came his quick reply. " Well, I don't want to go back!"

At least most of me, 75 to 80% I would say, did not want to go back.

Now the Angel spoke to me for the LAST TIME!

"YOU MUST GO BACK PETER." "IT'S NOT YOUR TIME AND YOU HAVE MANY IMPORTANT THINGS TO DO!"

With that very short but all powerful statement, the Angel now departed from me, and was gone. Gone, as if he had never been there at all. But he had most definitely been there and had made this all IMPORTANT statement to me!

I was now left at the ceiling by myself to ponder the situation, the Angel had left me with! I guess I don't have any more say on this matter, my thoughts.

I wish the Angel would come back and tell me more, because there was so much more that I wanted to know. So much more that I needed to know.

What kind of important things did I have to do that the Angel was talking about anyways? He never said and he never gave me a chance to ask him either. I guess I'll just have to wait to find these things out for myself.

That's if I'm able to survive this terrible illness!

A Special Angel/Human CONNECTION Now UNCONNECTED!..............

In one quick move, quite a bit different from when I had exited my body, I was now back inside it once again. My mother was sitting next to my bed, holding my hand, with a worried look on her face.

I now attempted to calm her.

"Mom, I don't think I'm going to make it, but don't worry, because everything is going to be alright." "Far more alright than you might even think!"Now she started to cry. Please don't talk like that, Dr. Kelly says you've got a fifty-fifty chance." "Well mom, Dr. Kelly may be wrong about this one." "Everything is going to be ok though, please believe me.

I'm now in the best hands I could ever want to be in."

"If I should die, just make the minimum of funeral arrangements and keep the rest of my insurance policy, ($10,000) because you need it."

"Why are you talking this way?" "You're not going to die."

Calmly I said; "Mom, if I should live, I'll tell you all about it, (which I did) but if I should die, it won't really matter." "Either way mom, everything is going to be more than ok, please believe me."

Mom gave me a kiss goodbye on the forehead, told me to get some sleep and that she would be back in the morning.

Now I was left alone to ponder this near death experience I had just went through and what it all meant.

All things considered, this had been quite a busy day, and I was completely worn out in the process. Which ever way this turns out, everything is going to be more then ok, my thoughts as I slowly drifted off to a much needed sleep!

A Body and Soul Reconnection Made!....................

Dr. Kelly was called out a few nights later, sometime around 2:30am to unclog the tubes in my nose that were draining my stomach. They had somehow gotten all clogged up, and the nurses on the night shift, couldn't seem to unclog them, so they called him in for his expert help.

On September 30th, nine days after the initial operation Dr. Kelly came in my room early in the morning to take the stitches out of my incision.

"It looks like we might have a big problem here Peter." "What kind of a problem Doc?"

"Peter, please ly back and try to relax a little." He took a small scalpel from a student nurse (Mary Clancy) classmate of mine and took a small specimen of the tissue from my incision.

I just about came out of the bed it hurt that much. It felt like somebody had just stabbed me in the stomach! The pain was so great, sweat began running down both sides of my cheeks.

"I'll be back later this afternoon Peter, please try and hang in there in the meantime." My incision was now starting to really hurt and I thought, somethings going on here and it doesn't bode well for me, not at all!

Now that I was back in my body, I was going to try and fight to stay there, the best that I could. I'm sure that's what we all would do, if given the same set of circumstances. Human nature, being what it is, we humans all try to somehow survive. Even the ones like me, who have seen Heaven!

Sometime around 5:30 that afternoon, Dr. Kelly came back in, and he brought some bad news with him! What more bad news could I possibly now have, my thoughts!

"Peter, I got the lab results back of your incision tissue I took this morning, and its not good!" "I'm going to have to take you back up to the operating room in the morning." "You have an abscess that has formed in your incision, and I need to clean it out and put some drainage tubes in to drain the poison, away from the site."

"Isn't there something else you can do Doc?"

"You basically have three choices Peter."

"And they are?"

"One, is to take care of the problem here in your room, without putting you to sleep, like this morning and you know how bad that hurt."

"That one is completely out of the question, Doctor Jim!"

"The second option and the best one is to take you up to the operating room, where I have everything to work with. I'll be able to put you to sleep, and take care of this abscess surgically and you won't feel a thing"

"And the third choice Doc?"

"You'll be dead in a few days!"

"Then I really don't have any choice at all, do I Doc?"

"No Peter, you sure don't!"

I thought, dear Lord, is there anything else that could possibly go wrong next? I was soon to find that one out too. The fourth day after the second operation, I developed double pneumonia! What a low blow this was!

If I had any luck at all in this year of 1960, it would be all bad!

While the Yankee's and Pirate's were playing the 1960 World Series, in the first ten days of October, I the ultimate sports fan was so severely sick and delirious, that I didn't even know who was playing and couldn't have cared less. I was one sick puppy!

However, I did win three pool's in the series, only because my nurses put me in the pools without my having any knowledge of it.

When I went into the hospital, back in the early morning hours of September 21st, I weighed 118lbs. When I left the hospital, twenty nine days later on October 20th I weighed just 79lbs. I had lost 39 pounds in 30 days!

Good Lord I thought, this must have been some kind of a record.

My mom said I looked like a refugee from a prisoner of war camp.

Believe it or not, I felt far worse than I looked, if that was possible!

It took me almost three long months to gain most of my lost weight back, plus all the strength that I had lost with it.

Thanks to God and my special Angel, I finally climbed out of that deep hole and eventually made it all the way back.

My total hospital bill, if you can believe it for the thirty days was $1,065.05!

There was also an $83.00 lab fee. Incredible to believe, compared to the cost of todays high medical bills!

A month later I got a bill from the hospital for $72.00 what the Travelers Insurance didn't pay. I took the bill down to the hospital and talked to the Nun in charge of the billing department.

I explained to her of my terrible situation with the apartment fire, getting bumped off my job, my inability to get any unemployment benefits, plus the fact I was in no condition right then to go back to work, not even as an extra railroad clerk.

At least, not until I gained some more weight along with much more of my strength back, which I hoped wouldn't be too long.

When she had heard it all, she finally spoke, telling me that she fully understood everything that was going on with me and thanked me for coming in and explaining it all to her. She told me not to worry. Just do the best I could when I was able to pay the bill. She added that the hospital would send me no more billings, since I had come in and talked to her about everything. I thought that was a nice gesture on her part!

I told her I would pay the bill off when I got my income tax return back in the Spring, if not before. I ended up paying the bill off long before the income tax refund came!

A Nun/Patient Connection…

My buddy Bob Egan asked me if there was anything else I could now possibly do or anyone I could now turn to, to aleviate my money problem.

"When I feel somewhat better, I have someone in mind that I'm going to try and ask for help." "I hate to do it, but I have no other choice."

In another month when I was feeling a little bit better physically, I went into the Mens Shop, a fine men's store on Main St., that was owned by two nice Jewish brothers, Nate and Max Landman.

I told them my situation of needing much clothing. I explained to them that I had no permanet job, no savings, no unemployment, no credit rating, but only my word to pay the bill back when I was able, which might be six months to a year. They asked me how much I would like to charge!

I thought between $250 and $300 ought to be more than enough.

As I recalled, the bill came to around $270, which was a good sum of money in those days. Especially for a young person with no job at the present time. Also no credit rating, but just my word.

It was really nice for someone to have faith and trust in you for a change!

Thank you Landman brothers for that trust!

A Mens Shop/Customer Connection!............................

I could finally see a light at the end of the tunnel. I would qualify for railroad unemployment if there was no work for me starting on February 19th of 1961 when I had been a railroad employee for one year! As it turned out by then I was making five days a week so it really didn't matter anymore!

When I got back to work sometime in early December of 1960 on the clerk's extra list, the Mens Shop bill was fully paid off by the the middle of 1961.

Before I could mark back up for work I had to take a railroad physical with Dr. Raymond Kelly, Dr. Jims dad. He took one look at me, weighing around ninety six pounds and asked what had happened to me, all the while checking on my incision wound at the same time. "Ruptured appendix, Doc!"

"So you must be the young man, my son has been telling me all about." "He told me you were way beyond lucky to live through the whole thing!

"He called it a miracle and after listening to everything he had to say concerning your case, I certainly would have to concur!"

"By the looks of this incision, it would seem the two of you have been having a lot of activity at this location." A laugh from both of us followed. "Not much fun for me Doc and I don't think much fun for Dr. Jim either!"

"I know Pete." "Are you absolutely sure you feel up to going back to work at this time?" "Not really Dr. Kelly, I sure don't feel much like it but I need the money in the worst way so I'm just going to have to suck it up and do it."

"I understand Pete and since its only a clerical job, I'm going to pronounce you fit for work, effective today." "Thank you Doc, I sure do appreciate it!"

"My son told me you had a lot of grit and I can see for myself just what he was talking about." "Please be careful though, with that incision, ok?" "Thank you Doc, I'll sure try."

A Doctor Father/Doctor son Connection!........................

Just so the bad luck of 1960 never seemed to end, I got a bill from a Hornell optician for $75 for eye glasses, that were purchased back in the fall of 1957 when I Was just seventeen. It seems my mother couldn't pay the bill and my father wouldn't, so in time I took care of that long ago bill too!

THE CANDY MAN

In late December of 1960, my pal Bob Egan came to me with a special favor. Since things were dead on the railroad at this time of year and I wasn't getting much extra work, he asked me, along with two of other friends, Norm Flaitz and Gary Crowley who had just gotten out of the army, to take him and Norm to Southeast, Florida.

Norm's mother was a waitress at the posh Fountainbleu Resort Hotel and had secured jobs for both Bob and Norm as bus boys at the resort.

Egan would pay me the expenses for gas and eats, both going down and coming back! His sister Shirley was a nurse there, so he had a place to stay. Norm of course had a place to stay with his mom!

I also thought that maybe the warm weather would help my incision to heal faster so I agreed to do it and help the two of them out. We left Hornell in early January, right after New Years Day for the trip south.

The four of us would take turns driving, so there wouldn't be any expense for a motel room. This was of course before U.S. 95 was built so we would have to take U.S.1 and U.S.301. These two main north-south routes were about fifty percent four lane and the other fifty percent two lanes. The big rub was that they both went right through all the villages, towns and cities that were in their path.

We left Hornell late in the afternoon of January 3rd.

In the early morning of our second day, I was driving somewhere in Maryland, when I noticed a red cadillac with its hood up parked along the shoulder of the road. Standing alongside of the car was a well dressed man in a suit. He seemed to be quite agitated. I pulled over on the shoulder of the road just ahead of him and walked back. "Am I ever glad to see you," was his greeting!

"What seems to be your trouble?" "I don't really know, but all of a sudden the car just started slowing down and finally came to a dead stop."

"I tried starting it back up, but it wouldn't even turn over!"

"I was able to get it off the road to the shoulder though, thank God!"

"This looks like a fairly new car." "It is." "Its brand new, just two weeks old." "I hate to tell you this, but It sounds to me like you might be out of gas." "Well, the gas gauge registers full." "When did you last get gas ?"

"Two weeks ago, when I bought the car." "Do you drive a lot?" "I sure do, I'm a candy salesman for Schraft Candies." "You probably have a defective gas gauge."

"There was a gas station about four or five miles back." "I'll take you back, get a couple of gallons of gas and that should solve your problem to get the car going again, ok?"

"You would trouble yourself like that for me?" "Yep, I sure would."

"No trouble at all!"

"If you do that for me, I'll sure make it right by you!"

"Don't worry about that!"

We loaded him up in the car and took him back the five miles to the gas station/restaurant, we had passed by just a little while before.

On the way back he asked us if we had breakfast yet? "No we haven't," came my reply. Back at the station, he told the proprietor to give him two gallons of gas and he would be back to fill up the gas tank in a short while.

He also told the owner to give us anything for breakfast that we wanted and put it on his bill. He would pay for everything when he came back.

While my three buddies went in to eat, I took the candy salesman back to his car with the gas. Once the car had gas in its belly, it started right up without any hesitation.

He said he had something special for me and would meet me back at the restaurant.

When we got back, he told me that more then a dozen cars had passed him by before we stopped and he was eternally grateful for us coming along and stopping.

He pulled out his wallet and gave me a brand new twenty dollar bill.

He then reached into his back seat for a large box of Schraft Candies.

I told him it wasn't necessary to do all of this, but he insisted!

His parting words to me as he pulled away were; "You were like an Angel to me, appearing out of nowhere." My words back to him were,

"Just glad to have been of some help!" As this story plays out, he was as much an Angel in the end to me as in the beginning, I was to him!

One Sweet Connection Here! And Another One Coming Up!...............

Egan's sister Shirley along with three other nurses rented a large house in Ft. Lauderdale. We stayed with them for three days and then Gary and I had to start back up north.

Just so connections never seem to cease is this little tidbit;

Gary set the basketball one game scoring record at Hornell High of 37 points in 1957. I was one point shy of his mark with 36 points in 1958. Two back to back basketball Connections together now!

Before leaving Ft. Lauderdale, I gassed up my car and we satisfied our appetite with burgers from a White Tower fast food restaurant.

After paying for the gas and the burgers, we had only twenty dollars left.

This was the twenty dollar bill the candy man had given me for assisting him a few short days before. This money would have to take us the 1,300 miles back to Hornell!

Always remember, The good that goes round, usually comes back round again! Not always from the same source, but it comes back from somewhere!

The candy man was about to be our Angel and we were going to be the assisted! Now A Reverse Connection!...........................

We left Ft. Lauderdale at 12:30pm. While going through Waycross, Ga. sometime around 8:30pm that evening, we spotted a soldier bumming along the road in the dark. Gary spoke up; " Pick that soldier up Pete!" "I just got out of the army myself, and I know how hard it is to catch a ride!"

I drove all night, Gary slept and I guess the soldier did too, because he never spoke much. He was headed back to his post somewhere around Columbia, South Carolina.

When we stopped for breakfast early the next morning, the soldier didn't get out of the car with us. I walked back and asked him if he wasn't hungry.

"Yes I am but I have no money." "Come on, I've got some money!"

Twenty bucks in 1961 lasted almost an eternity.

For sixty nine cents you could have two eggs any way, bacon, sausage or ham, toast or an english muffin, juice, and coffee or milk.

And all that for just $.69. WOW!

Gas in Florida and Georgia was seven cents a gallon. In the Carolina's it was nine cents while back in Hornell it was a whopping fourteen cents!

When we arrived back home, I had a little less than a quarter of a tank of gas left and thirty seven cents. If we had had any car trouble at all we would have been cooked! Now, you tell me who the Angel ended up being!

IMPOSSIBLE to make this stuff up!

A   Double   Angel   Connection   Had   Now   Been Forged!.........................

DR. JAMES R. KELLY - PART II
A ONE TWO PUNCH!

One morning in late January of 1961, I received a call around 9:00am from Dr. Kelly's receptionist. Doctor Jim would like to see me in his office at 12:30pm that afternoon if I could possibly make it on such a short notice.

I told her, "I'll be there on time, if not a little bit before."

I had sprained my right ankle pretty bad while playing basketball at the Y the night before, and one of my buddies had driven me down to the St. James Hospital for an X-ray of the ankle and foot. The Nun, who was called in, to take my X-ray said "Dr. Kelly's office will be in touch with you Peter!" So this phone call must be for the follow-up with Dr. Kelly, concerning my sprained ankle/foot, from the night before or so I thought anyways.

Was I ever in for TWO big surprises, back to back this day!

As soon as I walked through the door into his office Dr. Kelly met me with this statement. "You have a high ankle sprain of your right ankle, so try and stay off it as much as you can for a couple of weeks, and it should heal just fine."

Now came a little lecture, along with a shake of his head. "What in God's name are you doing playing basketball anyways with that incision still open and seeping blood and puss!"

"Oh by the way Doc, not to change the subject, but I got a bill from your office a couple of days ago for $75 that the Traveler's Insurance didn't pay." "Do you have the bill with you Peter?" "Yeah I sure do." "I just want to let you know I probably won't be able to pay it until late spring or early summer."

"At least not until I get some more extra work in on the railroad, but please believe me, I will eventually pay it."

"Let me see the bill, Peter."

I reached in my pocket and handed it to him. He looked at it for a very short time, then tore it into a few pieces, while throwing it in the waste basket, at the same time saying, "I guess that takes care of that, doesn't it Peter." "Thanks Dr. Jim, I sure do appreciate it."

"As busy as you are Doc, did you call me in here just to tell me about my ankle sprain?" "No Peter, there are a couple of other things concerning you and me that I'm pretty perplexed about!" "I would like to go over these two things with you, if you have the time and don't mind."

"Its fine with me, Dr. Jim, I have all kinds of time today, so fire away!"

"First of all, who is the other Doctor you have other than me?" "You're the ONLY Doctor I've had for the last few years, but why do you ask?"

"Well, Peter you have had a broken right foot sometime in the past, that showed up on the latest X-ray of your foot." "The X-ray showed it has healed perfectly." "Since it has healed so well and since I've never put a cast on your foot, some other doctor must have put one on you." "I've never had a cast of any kind on either of my feet Dr. Jim." "Peter, you had to have a cast on that foot for it to have healed so well!"

This got me to thinking. "Is it at all possible to tell approximately when this broken foot might have occurred?" "Yes, I would say sometime about three years ago, somewhere in the vicinity of late 1957, probably sometime in December of that year!"

"I remembered spraining my foot real bad, or at least, I thought, it was a sprain, sometime in early December of 1957, one afternoon near the end of high school basketball practice." "After taking a shower, I hobbled the two short blocks home." "While my mom made dinner, and afterwards that evening, I kept my foot in a bucket of ice water which helped immensely in keeping the swelling down." "The soreness and discomfort in the foot lingered until it completely healed, sometime in early June of 1958, near the end of track season."

"What I thought, back then was a sprain, must have been a broken foot and I never even realized it." "Did you have an X-ray taken of the foot at the time, it happened?" "No sir Doc, I sure didn't." "I Probably should have, but I didn't." "It seemed like I was forever spraining my ankles or feet often, while playing ball, so I thought this was just another sprain."

"Ok, that may have happened, but what did you do to the foot, for it to heal without a cast?" "I remember buying three or four ace bandages at the time from Cards (a drug store) and kept the foot tightly wrapped with one of the ace bandages most all of the time." "I take it then, that you didn't put any pressure on the foot, did you?" "Well yeah, I sure did!" "I played games and practices with the team and never missed one day."

"After basketball season was over, I ran track too." "Gosh Pete, it must to have hurt didn't it?" "Well, yes Doctor Jim, it did hurt, but I didn't want to stop playing."

Shaking his head, from side to side in total disbelief, he continued.

"Well, Peter I've heard just about everything now." "You should never have put any pressure on that foot at all, at least not without a cast on it."

"I am completly amazed it healed at all, let alone so good."

"I have a confession to make Dr. Jim." "At first I was only wearing an ace bandage for practice and games, but it got to hurting me so bad, I had to wrap it continually. Once I did this sometime in mid January, the pain seemed to decrease quite a bit."

"Hard for me to believe Peter. I've known all along you had grit, but not this much!" "You just seem to will yourself through everything." "Unbelievable!"

He then proceeded to examine my incision wound to see how that was coming along. After the drains had been taken out, following my second operation on October 1st, the incision area was allowed to heal from the inside out, without any stitches. This procedure was done, just in case of the formation of any more abscesses, which I did end up having.

"It looks pretty good right now Pete, but it is still draining quite a bit and it probably won't be fully healed a hundred percent, until sometime in late March or early April, at the earliest."

"I wish you would do me and yourself a big favor though and stop playing ball until then." "I know that's probably asking way to much of you!" "If you put to much pressure on the incision, it could get much worse and start to reopen more and we sure don't want that to happen."

"What's the other thing you wanted to talk to me about Doc?"
"Peter, Is it ok with you if we talk about your ruptured appendix.?"
"If your not comfortable with it, I'll drop the subject altogether." When your twenty years old, nothing seems to faze you so my reply was, "Its ok Doc." "I'm fine with talking about it."

Now he abruptly hit me with this statement!
"By all rights Peter, we shouldn't even be having this conversation!"
"By all rights, you shouldn't even be here." "Really?" "I don't mean in this office, I mean on this earth, period!" "Oh, and by the way, before I forget it, I want to apologize to you and your mom for falling back to sleep on that night, that your mom called me up and took you down to the hospital."

"That's ok Doc, that could happen to anyone." "When I found out how bad things were with you, I felt terrible that I had fallen back asleep which not only complicated matters for me, but more important then that, complicated everything for you, including quite possibly your life."

"By the time I got to you in the operating room, you were just too far gone." "Way to much peritonitis(poison) had set in and had spread throughout your system, disrupting all the important organs in your body."

"I would say your appendix had been ruptured for twenty to twenty four hours, maybe even up to thirty hours." "In medical terms, way too long a time for any doctor to be of much help to you."

"Your window of opportunity to survive had long since closed."

"I did the best I could under the circumstance and closed you up."

"It's a complete miracle, that you survived the first operation let alone everything else that followed!" "Its really quite remarkable that you are here to talk about it today." " I really don't know of any other words to explain it, other than to call it a pure miracle."

"I didn't give you the chance of a plugged nickel of surviving, it was just that bad Pete!"

"I'm sure that God was in your corner on that day, Peter"

"And in your corner too Dr. Jim."

"I feel Your grit and dogged determination helped you through this terrible ordeal Pete." "You never seemed to give up and just seemed to will yourself to pull through it!" "I've never seen anything like it in my life!"

"I told your mom and grandmothers you had a fifty-fifty chance, but with all my medical knowledge along with my experience as a surgeon, you really had very little or no chance at all."

Doctor Jim was now smiling. "By the way Pete I can do a little plastic surgery on that incision when it finally closes to make the scar look a whole lot better once it is fully healed."

"You might have a gal see that scar and run the other way."

A laugh from both of us followed. "Thanks but no thanks, Dr Jim. I've had enough surgery for a while."And if a girl doesrn't like me because of this scar, all I can say is that she can keep right on running!"

A slight chuckle from both of us followed!

I never told him about my NDE, because by this time, I had clammed up on the subject and wasn't talking about it anymore to anyone. Oh, how I wish now that I had told Dr. Jim all about it. He probably would have been more confused then he already was. Maybe not!

I'm sure he would have listened to me and he wouldn't have just brushed me off, like so many others did.

He might have even understood the real reason for my survival, if he believed the Angel's words!

The Connection, I believe would have then come full circle;

God, Dr. Kelly and Me, A three Way Connection!............

Dr. Kelly didn't know it at the time, nor did I, but in a little more then two weeks, that incision was going to reopen and it would be seeping a whole lot more blood and pus. It wouldn't be all from playing basketball either.

At least not from basketball alone! There would be one other mitigating factore Connected with it! A huge storm plus a romp in a snowy field!

I walked out of his office, thinking, WOW!

I played my big game with a broken foot and didn't even know it.

If I had had a cast on the foot, that game would never have happened, at least not for me. The Batavia comeback game either! The Canisto scrimmage too!

And it was a pure miracle, according to Dr. Kelly, that I was even alive.

Dr. Jim had hit me with a one, two punch to my mid-section!

It sounded like I had been keeping my Angel pretty busy.

Oncd again,you can't make this stuff up!

One Large Doctor Jim/Peter Connection Here!...............

My thoughts; Thank you Dear Lord for watching out for me, and bringing me through everything, and also thank you for guiding Dr. Jims hands!

Time now, was running a little short for me. In just a matter of a few days, the first of the many important reasons, stated by my Angel for my remaining here on earth, was going to be put to the test. I had no inkling whatsoever of it happening, but it was comming and it was going to come in the dark of midnight, during a raging blizzard!
A Dark And Foreboding Field Connection Now Loomed Dead Ahead!.........

As a footnote, Dr. Kelly said I would probably have a lot of arthritis in my right foot in later years. Though I have arthritis in my shoulders, neck and rib cage from time to time, my foot, however, is doing just fine. Thanks be to God for ace bandages coupled with His healing hand!........

IN A BLIZZARD AT MIDNIGHT

Sue Furlong was a fifteen year old Sophomore at Hornell High School. She was going up to Galbo's Roller Skating Rink, just outside of town, for an evening of fun. Her father, William "Duke" Furlong, was an engineer on the Alleghany Division of the Erie Lackawanna Railroad, based out of Hornell.

I often called Duke for work, so I knew him well. He dropped her off at Galbo's sometime around 7:00pm and would pick her back up later, at 11:00pm, when the roller rink closed.

She looked and dressed much older for her age and at 5'7," she could easily have passed for nineteen or twenty instead of fifteen, going on sixteen. Even though the weather forecast was calling for heavy snow with possible blizzard conditions, she wore only a winter coat, along with loafers. She had no hat, boots, or gloves. Since she was going to the rink and coming from the rink in a car, she figured she wouldn't need them! Bad decision!

She didn't realize it at the time, but as it turned out, this would be one big mistake on her part, for later on that evening.

When this terrible ordeal was finally over, she gave two very conflicting stories of what actually happened to her.

One scenario was totally and completely unbelievable.

The second version was quite plausible.

The first rendition was this; some guy, who she met, while at the roller skating rink, forced her into his car, all by himself, while she was standing outside the rink waiting for her father to come and pick her up.

And with over two feet of snow on the ground to boot!

This version was way too far fetched to even consider. I think she made it up to escape the wrath of her father, for not waiting for him to come and pick her up at the designated time!

The second version was much more to the truth of what actually took place. While skating, she met this guy for the first time.

They skated together, and when the rink closed, he offered her a ride home. She accepted, deciding not to wait for her dad to come and pick her up.

This turned out to be a huge mistake on her part, one that she would come to deeply regret!

Instead of taking her home, he drove her to this remote area of East Avenue Extension, that Connected with the main road to Canisteo.

He stopped the car and while trying to put the make on her, or whatever, she jumped out of the car, along with her roller skates that were in a skate suitcase.

He then drove off, leaving her standing in the middle of the road, with a full blown blizzard in progress. Just to hard too even contemplate, doing to someone!

There were three or four homes down the road, about a half of a mile away, but at this late hour of the night, coupled with a roaring blizzard going on, they were all dark.

Thinking that this character might come back, Sue headed straight for the lights and safety of the fast freight yard office, in the eastbound rail yard.

Her dad worked there from time to time, so she was familiar with the area too! She knew there would be safety for her there!

To get there though, she would have to traverse an open field of about a half of a mile or so. In her way of thinking, if this jerk did come back, he would not follow her in a car, across this farmers field, with over two feet of snow in it, plus much deeper drifts. All things considerred, she probably was half scared to death of the situation she had now gotten herself in.

I was due in the westbound yard office at midnight as the third trick yard clerk. On this February night I was still oozing blood and pus from the incision of my second operation, back on October 1st. It would not completely close up and fully heal, until sometime in late March.

The incision site was covered with a sterile gauze pad and hospital strength adhesive tape. I carried some extra pads and tape in my shirt pocket inside my jacket, just in case, I needed them! I didn't know it, but just in case would end up being, a couple of hours away, on this dreadful night!

Way much sooner than I ever thought I would need them!

I had decided to go down to the YMCA this night and play a little basketball from 7:00 to 9:00 before going to work.

In my medical condition, along with the impending storm, not a very good choice on my part. When your young though, you think your invincible and can do anything, so I was going, even though better judgment on my part should have prevailed.

If my old girlfriend was still in my life, I would have caught the devil from her! She would have been all over me! Don't you just hate it when women are right, which is most of the time!

At 5:30pm the ground was completely bare with hardly a trace of snow.

Bad weather, however had been forecast for our area of western New York, all day long, for mid to late afternoon and on into Friday morning.

The forecast was for upwards of a FOOT or MORE of snow possible, with winds of 20-25 mph, and worse yet, possible low wind chill temperatures coupled with WHITEOUT conditions, causing little or no visibility! Ugh!

That forcast would have scared a polar bear!

As it turned out, everything would end up being TWO TO THREE times worse then had been predicted. At 5:45pm it was just starting to snow and it was coming down with a vengeance.

By the time I walked into the Y an hour later, the snow accumulation was already between four to five inches deep and snowing harder than when it started.

Leaving the Y over two hours later at 9:20pm, the weather was now quickly deteriorating, as if it could get any worse! The snow flakes seemed as big as nickels. With the temperature now falling quickly, the wind chill factor was also heading south, fast! Visibility was now down to zero!

It seemed like you were inside one big snow shaker!

The snow was well over a foot deep and was now coming down sideways.

It really was, because the winds were howling something fierce and had now shifted into overdrive, causing the snow to fall sideways.

The wind gusts were now up to thirty five to forty mph.

Unreal conditions to try and deal with! Just trying to walk and keep your balance in this awful storm was one huge chore in itself.

I had no way of knowing it, but in a very short time, just over two hours to be exact, I would be faced with a much larger challenge to deal with, if that was at all possible. Its time was now almost upon me!

When I left home for work some two hours later at 11:15pm the snow accumulation was now half way up my thigh, or a little over two plus feet and it was snowing just as hard, if not harder then when it had started, almost six hours ago!

The wind was now blowing a gale and the accompanying wind chill it was creating was now brutal!

The temperature was right around 10 degrees, and still going down!

The worst thing to me though was the wind chill factor, which was now fluctuating between minus 9 and minus 20 degrees depending on the wind speed, with terrible whiteout conditions, just for good measure!

Scraping the snow and ice off of my windshield, was all that I could barely do, before heading off to work.

There was also a need to clear the snow off of the hood and trunk of the car, just to be able to see what was ahead and behind me, such was the snow depth.

The windshield wipers were having a hard time keeping up with the snow and ice accumulation that was piling right back up on the windshield!

There was hardly any traffic at all on the roads on this night, which was one good thing. Most people, at least the smart ones anyways, knew enough to stay in their homes during a storm such as bad as this one was.

This night is sure going to be one for the books, my thoughts.

Little did I know just how bad this night would finally end up being, or thanks to God, the way it would mercifully end.

After I cleaned the snow from my car and finally got in, I felt a grabbing sensation near my incision site. Holy moly, my thoughts

This was more than a little twinge now and one that I didn't like at all. Hopefully it will go away, my thoughts.

I now tried to bargain with God!

Please Lord, help this pain and discomfort to go away, at least for this terrible night. I'll try to be good in the future and not play any more ball at the Y for awhile. At least not until this incision finally heals. That's a promise!

Believe it or not, It was a promise I ended up keeping!......

I had to get back out of the car and monkey with the wipers again because of the buildup of ice on them, making them all but useless!

Cleaning the snow off of the car took a little bit more out of me than I thought it would. I was completely exhausted from all the added exertion and also from the added strain that had been placed on my incision site.

To get to the Westbound Yard Office you had to leave town on Hart St., a two lane road, go up a steep hill, turning to your right onto what was called the back road to Canisteo. After driving along the side hill for about a half a mile, you had to make a sharp right hand turn onto a farmers dirt road and go down a very steep hill into the westbound yard parking lot.

It was tough enough to negotiate in the dark, in good weather. It would be impossible to even try to attempt it, under these extreme conditions.

Even if I was lucky enough to get down there, how would I ever get out in the morning, were my thoughts. It would be completely impossible!

I put that option out of my head right away!

While driving down East Main St. I decided my best plan of attack this night, would be to cross the tracks at East Avenue, at the west end of the eastbound yard and park in the cripple yard parking lot. I would be parked on level ground, which was good.

The only bad thing was that it would require a three hundred yard walk from there to the westbound office in almost hip deep snow. I wasn't happy about that proposition at all, especially with my incision really acting up now, but this was the only option left for me, at least on this brutal night.

I guess I could have marked off, but marking off was NEVER in my DNA. Not then, not now, not ever, not as long as I could possibly help it.

Railroads were always a 24/7/365 proposition, come the devil or the deep blue sea, and that would include this horrific night too.

Somehow I'll just have to suck it up and tough this night out, my thoughts.

Trackmen were always called out in bad snow storms like this, to clear a path for the yard switchmen and also to keep all the switches clear of any ice or snow accumulation, that would build up. And this storm was a duzy!

Not a particular good vocation, especially on a night as bad as this one was.

Thank God they had been here not too long ago and had shoveled out a good switching lead path. Bur since the snowfall was coming down extremely hard, coupled with the bitter high winds, it was filling right back in, almost as quickly as they were clearing it away.

In any event, It was really tough slogging for me. To top it all off, my incision site, was really starting to pain me now. This was more than a twinge, and had now become a semi-constant throb. The pain seemed to be getting worse, the further I walked, but there was no way I was turning back now, my thoughts!

The sands of time had just about run out of my hour glass and were almost gone! The first test of the Angels strong message to me was now just minutes away!

MY LAST thoughts were, darn it, why did I ever venture out in this storm to play ball tonight.

All things considered, I shouldn't have even been outdoors on such a night as this was! Certainly not in my condition anyways, let alone playing ball. What an idiot!

My girlfriend always said I was bullheaded and stubborn. I guess on this terrible night, she would have been right on, as she usually was, if only she had known.

But then, looking back in hindsight, wasn't she always right, or at least most of the time anyways……If only I had listened to her more, if only………..

It was now Midnight! THE BEWITCHING HOUR WAS FINALLY HERE! It was now time for me to rise up and get in the game!

My grit and determination were about to be tested to their farthest limits!

A Blizzard Connection Was About To Commence!...................

Suddenly, without any warning, I was jolted wide awake from my drifting thoughts by a loud piercing scream, followed by "God help me, won't somebody, please help me!"

My first thought was, this has got to be some kind of a terrible joke.

This was no kind of a night for this sort of shenanigans, my thoughts!

The voice however, sounded like that of a female, so that did give me a little pause in my way of thinking. Maybe this wasn't a prank after all.

Maybe someone really did need help, but where were they and what kind of help did they require?

The voice was coming off to my right in one of only two possible places!

Either a huge farmers field, that was used for grazing cattle in good weather, or East Avenue Extension on the far side of the field, a road that Connected with the main road to Canisteo, which was about one mile away.

Was someone in a car accident? Was a car broke down or stuck in a snow bank? Or was this just one terrible sick joke, my thoughts.

In the pitch darkness of night, along with a blizzard pummeling me from all sides, I couldn't tell for sure, but NO ONE and I mean NO ONE could be out in that farmers field. Surely not at this time of night, coupled with this brutal blizzard. Or so I thought anyways.

Was I ever in for one big surprise before this night was over!

You could only see about four to five feet in front of you, at best.

TOTAL WHITEOUT conditions were all around us now!

Voices however, seemed to carry, quite a long way. At least to me, they did.

Since the voice seemed to carry so well, maybe it was from East Ave. Extension, a long way off. Thats probably it, my thoughts!

In any event, I kept plugging along down the switching lead, but it was a supreme struggle and it was tiring me out right down to my bones.

The voice screamed again, "Can't anyone hear me, please somebody, anybody help me."

The voice, I now figured was coming from somewhere in the middle of the field. But on this night, with these terrible conditions, how could that be possible. Nah, this just couldn't be, my thoughts. If they were there, why were they there and how did they get there in the first place?

Come on now Pete, this seems too impossible to even consider, were my thoughts! With these terrible conditions, its just so hard to really tell!

Could it be possible their car broke down or got stuck in the snow on East Ave. Extension, and then they got disoriented in this God awful storm.

In this blizzard, on this night, almost anything is possible, my thoughts.

Maybe I'm just imagining the whole thing. Maybe, I just don't know for sure! I kept moving along, and my incision was now giving me fits to boot!

The throb had now become one constant ache. I was now pretty worried about this development on top of everything else, I was having to contend with! All the while I kept trying to move along just the same.

The switching lead was widening out now, going from two running tracks into eighteen yard classification tracks.

Looking off to my right toward the service road and the field, I could just barely make out the lights of a small car, stuck in a large snow bank, alongside the road.

It was four or five tracks over toward the service road, from where I was now standing.

Someone yelled out. "Pete is that you?" It was Julius Colleta, a fellow clerical employee of mine. He was the midnight Hump Yard clerk.

I could just about make him out.

His brother had brought him to work and now the brother's little Volkswagen Beetle was hung up in a huge snow drift and they needed help to get the car unstuck. "Yeah, its me Julius."

"Can you come over and help us?" "My brother's car is stuck!"

"Sure thing Julius, I'll be right there, just as soon as I can get there!"

The two of us pushed and pushed and finally rocked the little car loose and it was finally free and on it's way.

While this minor problem was being taken care of, the voice yelled out once again, and was now pleading, begging once more for help.

Any help, from anyone that could hear her. I could hear her alright but I needed some kind of confirmation, from someone else, that I wasn't just imagining all of this!

Can't anyone else hear this voice tonight other than me, my thoughts.

After all, many men other then me were showing up at this time of night for work. Some were also going off duty too.

Was the wind and the other conditions that bad, that no one other than I could hear her pleadings? How could It be possible I was the only one?

Am I so overwhelmed and so drained by this miserable storm that maybe, just maybe, I'm imagining the voice itself and everything that's Connected with it!

Maybe this voice I'm hearing isn't really happening at all.

Maybe this is all a mirage caused by the whiteout conditions, along with the crazy howling wind, coupled with me being so tired out! I'm just so gol darned confused with the whole incident!

Am I that exhausted that my mind is now playing tricks on me too.

I seem to be all confused with what my head is telling me and what my heart is hearing. My head says no one could possibly be out in that field in this terrible storm, at this time of night. Yet my heart is saying something far different! Its telling me that someone is out there and they need help!

Lord, please help me sort all this out, were my thoughts.

Now the voice was pleading, once more for help! "Please, can't somebody, anybody hear me?" "God, please help me!"

"Jule, I'm pretty sure there is someone, possibly a young woman over in that farmer's field, who needs our help."

"Don't you hear her crying out for help?" "Are you crazy or what Pete?"

"I don't hear anything at all, other then this awful wind, screaming at us all the while." Even with a warm winter jacket, scarf, gloves, hat and a hood, the conditions were unbelievably brutal. You had to face away from the direction the wind was blowing, just to be able to catch your breath.

This was not easy either, because in addition to the wind blowing, it was also swirling all around us at the same time.

Just unbelievable conditions to try to cope with!

Julius broke the silence once more. "Pete, on a night like this, you must be losing it completely to even think that someone could be over in that field!" "Are you sure this storm hasn't got to you Pete?" "I'm alright, Jule." "And I'm not crazy either!" "I'm not saying you're crazy Pete, but there's no one over in that dark field tonight, please believe me!" I was not about to give up on what I had been hearing on my tortuous trek, even if no one else could back me up on it! I was determined more then ever now to find out for SURE if someone was really out there as I was starting to believe more and more they were!

"I'm telling you Julius, even if it is hard for you to believe, there is someone over in that field!" "You'll see, just watch this!"

I now took my gloves off, cupped my hands and yelled out toward where the voice was coming from. "Where are you?" No answer or sound at all was now forthcoming.

I felt like a complete jerk. I guess I fell for this sordid joke, my thoughts.

"See Pete, nobody is out there." "It's just not humanly possible on a night like this, and why would they be out there anyways?"

"It must be just the wind your hearing Pete, its blowing a gale!"

Julius grabbed me by my shoulder turning me completely around to get to our jobs which were still about seventy five yards for him and a hundred fifty yards away for me.

Just then she screamed once more, only this time much louder than ever before. It was almost like an animals dying screech.

This time It startled me so much it even made me jump!

"Now Julius, you must have heard the voice that time, didn't you?"

"You know what Pete, I think I did hear something that time, but its got to be someone playing a prank, or quite possibly its just this awful wind, don't you think?" "Its no prank Julius and it's not the wind either, my friend."

"I am now totally convinced, there is someone definitely over in that field and it's a female." "I have no idea what she's doing out there, or how she got there but for whatever the reason, she needs our help and she needs it asap!"

"Look Julius, you go up to the fast freight (eastbound yard office) and get some more help. Maybe two or three other guys, will do."

"Oh and by the way, have Don Logan (the eastbound yardmaster) call Bob Bishop (the westbound yardmaster) and tell him I'm going to be a little late for work, but that it's an emergency and it can't be helped."

Since it was now 12:12am, I was already twelve minutes late for work.

I would not reach the westbound office this night until 1:25am.

"In the meantime, Julius I'm going over in that field."

"Right now, by your self Pete?" " Yes Julius, by myself, whats the big deal?"

"I dunno Pete, why not wait for me to go and get some more help." "That field looks so dark and foreboding to me."

"No Julius, this can't wait any longer." "In fact, its already waited way too long!" "I just had to be positive before I went traipsing out there in that field on a wild goose chase, especially in my condition!"

"Someone is in big trouble out there, and I'm going for them right now!"

"Don't worry about me Julius, just do as I tell you and go and get some more help, because I'm sure we're going to need them."

"I'll meet up with you out in the field in a little while, ok." "Ok Pete, but please be careful."

We then split up, Julius for the eastbound yard office about 150 yards away and me for the field right next to the service road………..

I climbed up and over the six foot fence that ran along the service road and dropped down to the other side, into the snow filled field. It was three to five feet deep in places where it had drifted and it was still snowing and blowing just as hard as ever. As deep as the snow was and it was up to my waist in places where it had drifted. I was totally amazed that I could almost actually run in it, It was so light and fluffy.

My adrenalin had also now kicked in, thank God!

I was now more wider awake then I had been all night, and I was now on a decided mission!

The voice, for some unknown reason, had now become totally silent, but I had a good bearing to where it had last come from, so that was no problem for me to head straight for it. The lights from the yard light towers helped illuminate my way too.

Even though starting out, I was dressed pretty warm, by now I was frozen half stiff from these awful conditions. The wind chill factor was much worse then all the snow. To me it was even beyond discription!

At about this time I felt something wet and warm running down my right pant leg. Pulling my leg up out of the snow to check, only confirmed what I had already figured it was and it was not good news!

Blood and puss were now seeping from my incision and were oozing a long red and yellow streak down my pant leg, soiling my pants! I can't stop now, my thoughts! Something deep inside me told me to just keep going, everything would be alright!

Within a few more steps, I got my left pant leg tangled up in a barbed wire fence. With all the deep snow, I never even realized it was there.

It ripped a gaping hole in my pant leg, cutting a deep gash to my left knee.

I was now some kind of a mess myself. These were good pants when I put them on this morning, but I would never wear them again, not after this night was over. They were now completely ruined......

After plowing through snow for another 75 yards or so, I finally reached Sue, who was now in a half sitting position, buried in snow right up to her head and neck. The whole scene, seemed so surreal. Looking all around me, I found it hard to believe this whole thing was actually taking place.

It felt like it was a scene that was being staged, but of course this was no movie! This was the real McCoy!

She had long blond hair, which was totally caked with snow and ice!

Her face and hands were beet red and felt so terribly icy cold to the touch.

I hugged her close to me for a minute and told her not to worry anymore, everything was now going to be alright!

She was just so cold and totally exhausted.

She was crying and could barely speak and worst of all she was shivering to beat the band. The first words that she whispered to me were "I'm so tired that I can't go on any further, but please don't hurt me."

"I'm not here to hurt you honey, I'm only here to help you."

"What are you doing out here anyways in this field, at this time of night, and in this God awful storm?" "It's a long story!" "What took you so long to get out here to help me?" "That's another long story too honey!"

"All that counts now though, is I'm here and your going to be alright!"

She was wearing a winter coat, but no gloves or hat, and she had lost both of her loafers somewhere along the way. She was now half barefoot with one sock on and one sock gone.

I took off my gloves and put her cold hands in them. I wrapped my scarf around her neck and tucked it in her coat, pulling her coller up.

After clearing cakes of snow or ice from her long hair, I put my baseball cap on her head. Believe it or not, she still had her roller skates in the skate suitcase with her and, they were anything but light.

"I'm just so tired, I can't go on any further!"

"I just want to go asleep." "No, you can't go to sleep!" "You'll never wake up!" "You've come way too far to quit now." "Don't give up!"

"Try to get up and move honey, I'll try and help you do it."

I then pulled her up in a full standing position and brushed a lot of snow off of her. She was a little taller then me at about 5'7". I could now see help coming from the fast freight yard office. Some of the men had lanterns. Thanks be to God, we're going to win this huge battle, my thoughts.

Julius and three yard switchmen finally showed up and they carried her out of the field.

Her feet were so cold that she had lost all feeling in them and was unable to walk any further on her own.

I went ahead with her skates and also to call for an ambulance (EMS today) to come and take her to the hospital to check her out for possible frostbite and/or exposure.

When we had her safely in the yard office and were warming her by the stove, she told of the two different stories relating to how she ended up in the car in the first place and eventually in the field.

The creep who was responsible for this dastardly deed was never found, at least, not to my knowledge anyways.

By the time I finally got to the westbound yard office at 1:25, all kinds of rumors concerning this episode were flying all around. One rumor was that I was helping some people out in a car accident on East Avenue Ext. Another rumor had it that I had gone home sick and hadn't even bothered to tell anyone. Yeah right, in your dreams, I thought!

One westbound yard switchman, Leon Barnaby, took one look at my torn and bloody pants and thought I had been in some kind of accident myself.

I cleaned up my incision wound and put some fresh gauze and tape on it.

I tried to stay off my feet for the rest of the night which made it feel a whole lot better too. I also throughly cleaned the gash on my left knee. No telling if the barbed wire fence was rusty, but I wouldn't have been surprised if it was.

It snowed hard all night and our building shook all night long, from the terrible wind conditions outside.

By 8:00am when the storm finally abated to just snow flurries, an incredible THIRTY-NINE INCHES of snow had fallen on the level in just a little over fourteen hours.

A great many of the drifts were between five to seven feet deep. One unbelievable storm to be sure!

It was truly a night I would never forget for the rest of my life in a lot more ways than one.

In the morning everyone had to walk home and leave their cars buried in the snow at work. Workers coming to relieve us, were also coming by foot. Cars do not operate very well in thirty-nine inches of level snow, plus so many deeper drifts.

Since I had to come right back in eight hours to work the 4:00pm shift at the eastbound fast freight office, I trudged over there and laid down on a mattress that was in the crew room and tried to get some sleep.

I was now completely and totally exhausted! My incision felt a whole lot better though, which was good and relieved my mind some.

At 12:30pm, Sues dad, woke me up and wanted to talk with me about her terrible ordeal from the night before. I was more than glad to tell him what I knew.

I asked him how she was doing and he told me. "Thanks to you Pete she's going to be all right." "She almost had some frostbite on one foot, the barefoot one, but the doctors says it should be ok."

"She told me she was completely out of gas and couldn't go on any further or even yell any more for that matter, when you finally reached her."

"Thank God you were there Pete, it's only a miracle she didn't die out there." "Everyone is saying you saved her life." "I helped Duke, I helped!"

"That's not what they're all saying around here Pete." "There calling you a hero and saying you saved her life!

"It seems that no one else around here heard anyhing out in that field last night but you!" "I know, its hard to believe, but thats what they're all saying!"

"So once again Pete, my heartfelt thanks." He put his arms around me and gave me a big hug.

I tried to go back to sleep for a few hours, but sleep of course would not come, not on this day, anyways. I guess I was too wired from the night before!

A Railroad/Field Connection!...........

In later yearas Sue was married to a classmate of mine, Frank Fenti.

They lived right around the corner from us on Sawyer St.

Just so Connections never seem to cease coming, Franks father, Lundy Fenti was the foreman of the trackmen the night of the blizzard and he was in the eastbound yard office, when we brought Sue in from the snowy field.

He didn't know Sue at the time but sometime down the road in the future, Sue was going to end up being his daughter in law!

Frank ending up dying with a heart attack sometime in his late forties or early fifties. Way to young!

Over the years, I lost track of Sue.

A SMOKING CAR

In April of 1965, my wife Jean and our two year old son Michael were living in an upstairs apartment at 22 ½ Maple St.

Barbara Rohan, a girl I went to school with, at Hornell High lived upstairs right next door to us, at 20 ½.

She had a boyfriend who I only knew as Joe, who worked somewhere in the construction trade.

He was a big man, of about 6'2" and weighed somewhere, I would guess in the vicinity of 220lbs. He seemed like a friendly enough guy and always spoke to me, whenever we chanced to meet.

When he was at Barb's place, which was almost every day, night, or both, he parked his car in the Acme Supermarket parking lot facing Maple St. and our place, instead of in front of Barb's apartment on the street.

They seemed to get along quite well together most of the time.

Just so Connections keep on coming, Francis Crowe, my good friend Billy Crow's father who got me my job on the railroad was Barb's Uncle.

Her mom and Francis's wife were sisters. Super nice ladies they were too.

Living next door to each other, we were separated only by a narrow driveway. With no air conditioning, the windows were always wide open in good weather. You could hear everything that was going on next door. Sometimes, a little more than you wanted to hear or needed to know.

This happened a good deal of the time. In fact, way too much of the time.

On this late balmy, Spring night, I had watched a baseball game earlier on TV and then switched over to a late night movie at 11:30pm, after the game and the late news were over. I fell asleep halfway through the movie, on the sofa in my underwear and didn't wake up until sometime around 1:40am. The only thing that was now showing on the TV was the test pattern.

This of course, was a few years before twenty four hour television was introduced. Having to relieve myself, I turned the television off, headed for the bathroom and then on to bed.

For some mysterious reason, I stopped to look out the kitchen window, which overlooked the Acme parking lot across Maple St. What I saw startled me wide awake. From my view, I could quickly tell a few things about the situation!

Joe's car was backed half way out of the parking slot and was stopped sideways. The car was running alright, but the gear shift must have been in park position.

The drivers side door was wide open and the car was quickly filling up with smelly black smoke, coming from somewhere under the hood.

It appeared that Joe was slumped over unconscious or worse, with his head resting directly on the steering wheel. To make matters worse, his head was tilted toward the passenger side, where most of the smoke seemed to be coming from.

Quickly I sprang into action, grabbing the phone.

"Number please," came the calm voice of the operator at the other end of the line. "Fire Department, right away," was my hurried reply.

Two rings and "Fire Department." "Come as quick as you can, there's a car on fire in the Acme parking lot facing Maple St."

"We're on our way," came the terse reply.

The car wasn't on fire as yet, but it was full of billowing putrid smoke and I feared it was only a matter of seconds before it would be engulfed in flames, with Joe in it. Maybe worse, Heaven forbid, the car might explode!

No way of telling from here how bad things really were!

Since I was only in a tee shirt and under shorts, I had to grab a pair of pants and shoes. I quickly dashed down the stairs and on the run, headed for the car.

On the way down, I was thinking, what am I gonna do when I get there?

I'm only 5'4" and 130 lbs. No way will I be able to do anything with Joe,

He's way too big for me to handle. Silently, I begged God for some assistance. Dear Lord, I need your help big time on this one!

As I arrived at the car, somewhere from deep inside me came a quick answer to my silent prayer, "You can do it Pete, so just do it."

Without any hesitation, I reached in and turned the ignition off.

Quickly now, I grabbed the back of Joe's shirt, pulling him up and over towards me, while turning his head completely around at the same time.

Mercifully, he was now facing away from the majority of the smelly smoke, and was now facing fresh air instead!

I then tipped him around backwards towards me, while at the same time, getting both of my arms under his armpits and pulled him out of the car. Surprisingly, he sort of just slid right on out of the car.

The move went a whole lot easier then I ever thought it would.

Amazingly, neither of his feet were entangled under or around the gas or brake pedals. That was one huge break for the both of us, my thoughts!

While all this was taking place, I was quite concerned, that the car was about to catch fire at any moment now and might engulf us both. At least not until I had gotten the both of us far enough away from the car!

I said a little prayer it wouldn't, for I was on a mission now and there would be no turning back!

I thought If it was gonna happen, it would have to get me too.

I'm thinking, now comes the hard part. Thank God, finally my adrenalin had now kicked into high gear!

With my forearms still under his armpits, I dragged him about thirty-five feet away from the car, all the while expecting it to burst into flames at any moment. He was all dead weight too, since he was completely unconscious, or maybe even worse, Heaven forbid! At the time, I wasn't quite sure of either!

The smoke seemed to be getting more raunchy and thicker with each passing minute. I wondered at this time whether Joe was dead or alive.

He didn't appear to be breathing and he was certainly unconscious or worse.

Not being that acquainted with CPR, I did what I could for him.

I loosened his belt and tried to breathe into his mouth until help finally arrived, which wasn't very long, since the fire house was only about a mile away.

The fire department was there real fast, in about ten to twelve minutes.

Two firemen extinguished the smoke from under the hood of the car before it could develop into a fire while two others put a breathalyzer on Joe as soon as they arrived.

After what seemed like an eternity, they restored Joe back to life.

It took around a full 10 minutes. One of the firemen, Roger Kramer said "It was a good thing you were here tonight Pete, you just saved this guys life."

"Ten more minutes of that smoke and we probably wouldn't have gotten him back." "In fact, we were very fortunate as it was!"

"By the way who helped you pull this guy out of his car and away from It?" "Nobody!" "Really!" "When the adrenalin kicks in Roger you can do a lot of things you didn't think you could do

otherwise." "The BIG GUY upstairs helped me too, of that I'm sure." "Something, deep inside of me told me to just do it, and so I did!"...
A Late Night Neighborly Connection Made!.....................

Since it was well after 2:00am by now, I headed back upstairs to home and to bed. The firemen took Joe home and had his car towed the next day! I didn't see Joe around much anymore after that night.
For one reason or another that was the end of their relationship.
In a few short years Barbara moved out to Arizona to live with a sister and died at a young age from some form of cancer!
A Sad Ending Connection!.............

BLOOD AND MUD

Bob Sullivan worked as a machinist/electrician at the diesel shops, in Hornell for the Erie Lackawanna Railroad. He, his wife and large family lived on Ontario St. I knew his wife too, because she worked at a couple of Elmhurst Dairy stores in Hornell that I frequented for bread, milk and ice cream. The official payday for the railroad was Thursday but if the checks were in early the night before, you could pick them up at the ticket office in the depot anytime after 6:00pm. on Wednesday evening.

Sully would always pick his check up early Thursday morning, his day off, go across Loder St. to a gin mill, cash his check and get smashed.

Every Thursday, with the exception of Thanksgiving and Christmas, just like clockwork.

I reported for work at the depot on Thursday through Monday as the mail room clerk and baggage handler. My tour of duty was 11:00am to 7:00pm with twenty minutes off for lunch. I always picked up my check on Thursdays when I showed up for work!

Matt Delaney was the Ticket Agent and Tom Hogan, the Chief Clerk.

Their hours of duty were 9:00am to 5:00pm with 20 minutes off for lunch. On the trackside of the depot ran the westbound and eastbound main tracks. Then came an open field for about 75 yards or so, to what was called ryans track, which was a busy freight running track into the eastbound yard.

Just beyond ryans was Depot St. Loder St. on the street side of the depot was named for a long ago president of the Erie RR, Benjamin Loder.

Depot St. was named for the depot I would guess, even if it was on the opposite side of the tracks from the depot.

Sully was a pretty nice guy when he wasn't drinking, but when he was in the suds, look out. He could be a hand full. He could be ornery as the devil and quite belligerent too. Especially after he had more than enough beer in him, which was just about every Thursday. I always reported fifteen minutes early for work at 10:45am and every Thursday morning. Sully would show up in the baggage room around 11:30am. You could almost set your watch by his arrival.

He could be soft and mellow, which wasn't very often to downright nasty. No telling which Sully would show up from Thursday to Thursday, but the majority of the time, I would say on the nasty side. Most of the time, I would just humor or ignore him and go about my work. Eventually he would get the message, leave and go home, sleep it off and that would be that.

At least until the next Thursday rolled around.

This cool, rainy, April, Thursday in 1967 was going to be a far more different day. There had been a heavy rain over night and now a steady drizzle was still falling, so everything was wet, damp, and muddy.

I had a sinus headache that wouldn't stop, so I didn't have a lot of patience with Sully on this day. When he started up with his nonsense, I said "Sully, do me a big favor today, and please just leave and go home!" "I have a splitting headache and I am not in the mood for your carrying on today, so please just go home."

"You don't have to get personal with me," was his curt retort.

"If that's the way you feel about it, I'm going to get out of here right now and never come back again." Yeah right, I thought, that'll be the day!

At least not until next Thursday anyways. "Whatever Sully, whatever, you think is best, but please go home for now, and I'll see you next week, ok."

"You won't see me next week or any other week for that matter." "I like you Pete, thats why I come around here, but I'm not going to come in here anymore to see you, so what do you think about that?"

"I'm sure going to miss you Sully, but please feel free to do whatever you think is best." "See you later, and be careful when crossing the tracks, that you don't slip, because its so wet out!" "You don't have to worry about me, I know how to cross tracks." "I worked on this pike long before you were even born." "Your right about that Sully." "I'm going now Pete, so goodbye and I won't be coming back either!" "See you later Sully." "No you won't!" "You won't see me ever again." "Now Sully, you know that isn't so!"

I watched as Sully went out the trackside door of the baggage room and navigated across the two main tracks. He seemed to steady himself a little bit as he walked the field toward ryans. When he started to step over ryans, he tripped over the nearest rail, and went down hard, face first on the far rail and ties. He tried to get up, but could only manage about 1/3 of the way up, before he collapsed face down and spread eagled right in the middle of the track and stayed there, passed out!

I ran into the ticket office to tell Matt and Tom about Sully's predicament. Much to my surprise, they had been watching the whole incident take place through the ticket office trackside window.

By the way, Tom was a pretty good drinker in his own right, as well as Sully. He wasn't called Nasty Tom, because he was a choir boy either!

Technically Matt was in charge of the office. Tom was second in command and I was third or way down on the pecking order.

Most of the time though, Matt let Tom take charge, as Tom was always want to do. He loved to run the show and exert his authority.

"Tom, I think Sully is hurt, maybe bad!" "We've got to go over there right now and get him up off ryans before an eastbound (freight) for the yard comes along and runs him over!"

"Leave him right where he fell," was Tom's quick reply.

"We're not going to do anything."

"Maybe your not going to do anything Tom, but I surely am."

"The devil you are mister, your not going any where either."

Oh but I am Tom!"

"I'm giving you fair warning Pete, if you go over there, your going to be out of service, so you had better think twice about it, before you do it!"

"You can't take me out of service for that." "It would never stick and you know it." "I'm giving you a direct order and you had better obey it, do you understand me?" Matt now chimed in. "You had better listen to Tom, Pete."

"Baloney Matt, no way am I gonna listen to Tom or you either, for that matter." "Not on this one anyways!"

"Now here's what we're going to do." "Tom, you take your car, go up and under the subway, and come down Depot St!" "In the meantime I'll go over and try to get Sully up off of ryans if I can, and we'll take him home." "That's If he's not hurt too bad. If he Is hurt bad, then we'll take him on down to the St. James." (Hospital)

Tom was completely beside himself now. Not only was I refusing his direct order, but I was the one now giving the orders of what we were going to do, concerning Sullys dilemma.

Tom didn't like it one bit, but I could have cared less! Sully needed someones help asap, and we were going to be that someone to come and help him, whether Tom was on board with it or not!

I was out the door in a flash and on the run toward ryans before Tom could utter another word.

Sully was not a large man by any strech, weighing around 160lbs.

But at 5'10" he was, a lot taller than me. When I got him up and off the track by myself, which wasn't very easy in his condition, I took a good look at his face.

He was a mess. He had a nasty gash across much of his forehead, just above his right eyebrow, that extended part of the way down the middle of his nose. It resembled a red sideways letter L. What wasn't blood on his face was mud. His clothes were pretty much covered with mud too.

A most peculiar thing. I never carried a handkerchief with me, but on this day when I needed one in the worst way, I had one. I didn't even remember putting it in my pants back pocket that morning. Quite surreal to say the least, on this count, my thoughts…

I cleaned the wound site on his forehead the best that I could and also wiped away mud off much of his face.

Thank God no eastbound freight had come along headed for the yard.

Much to my joy and amazement, Tom was there in a few short minutes. Was he ever livid, which I fully expected him to be, if he even bothered to show up. I got Sully loaded in the back seat and jumped in the passenger front seat.

Tom was so mad, you could almost see the steam, coming out of the top of his head.

"Your in big trouble mister when we get back to the depot."

"I don't think so Tom." "Just you wait and see mister, just you wait and see." "In fact you can consider yourself out of service as of right now."

"Your making a big mistake on this one Tom."

"I'll write up the paperwork when we get back to the depot!"

Tom was really pushing things hard now. He was not about to let me unsurp him, not in a heartbeat. It just wasn't going to happen, not if he could help it anyways.

"You ignored my direct order to not get involved in this thing!"

"It was the right thing to do Tom!"

"Its still insubordination!" ""I don't care Tom, it was the right thing to do, and the best part, you know it, or should know it!"

"Tom, not to change the subject, but don't you, Matthew and Sully all go to the same church, St. Ignatius?"

Connected

"Yeah we do, so what difference does that make?"

"None I guess, I was just asking." "Well, don't ask and don't talk to me anymore either."

Tom and I got Sully out of the back seat and walked him up to his front door and rang the door bell. Mrs. Sullivan must have seen us coming because she answered the doorbell almost immediately.

Taking one look at Sully, she blurted out, "Oh Sully what has happened to you?" Looking over at Tom, she continued. "Oh Tom, thank you so much for looking out for Robert and bringing him home safely."

"You don't know how much I appreciate it."

Then looking over at me, "Hi Pete, how are you?" "I'm good Mrs. Sullivan, thank you!"

Tom was getting ALL the credit for rescuing Sully up off of ryans and bringing him safely home, when he didn't want to even lift one little finger to help him and worse yet, he didn't want me to get involved in helping him either.

Yes I thought, this is one sweet moment to savor! I was tickled pink with this outcome, because now, with Tom being given all the credit for the rescue, what more could he possibly say to me about insubordination or anything else that was Connected with this matter.

You gotta love it, my thoughts. Tom's over a barrel and the best part of it is he knows it, and he doesn't like it, not one bit.

God sometimes does work in mysterious ways, my thoughts!

Needless to say, Tom and I didn't speak at all on the ten minute ride back to the station. When we got back, Tom went into the ticket office and I went back to what I was doing in the baggage room.

Nothing more was ever said between us concerning Sully's ordeal.

Tom didn't speak to me for a few days, but that was more than ok with me!

After we started talking to each other once again I sensed Tom and I had a better relationship then before. I think he respected

149

me for taking a stand to do what was right to rescue Sully up off of ryans, but he never said as much!

Another Field Connection Made!.................

A couple of related stories pertinent to this incident;

Sully didn't come to the baggage room the following Thursday, like he usually did and I was worried whether or not he was ok. I sure hoped he was, because I really liked Sully. I also hoped he wasn't still mad at me.

However he did show up on the second Thursday, but at 11:00 instead of his usual time of 11:30 and on this day he was stone sober.

"Pete, I just wanted to stop by to see you and to thank you so much for being there for me and helping me out a couple of weeks ago, like you did." "By the way Pete, I'm also real sorry for giving you such a hard time that day too!" "That's ok Sully, no problem there!"

"How is that gash over your eyebrow and nose coming?" "Its coming along real good Pete."

"My wife told me Tom Hogan had brought me home after I had fallen down on ryans. I told her hogwash, it wasn't Hogan at all, it was Pete, who was there and was looking out for me!"

"In fact, I told her that I heard Hogan tell you he was going to take you out of service and all because of helping me."

"I was just glad to have been of some help to you Sully."

"You were a lot more than some help Pete, please believe me." "I could have gotten myself killed over on ryans."

"You quite possibly might have saved my life!"

"What's up with you Sully, no drinking today?" "No, I've decided to turn over a new leaf." "So I guess I'll see ya around, unh Pete?" "Right Sully, be good, and I'll see you around too."

With that he walked out the trackside baggage room door and across the tracks for home. I watched him go until he was clearly out of sight.

I would be lying if I denied that I had to wipe a few tears from my eyes.

Yes, I thought, Bob Sullivan was going to be just fine.

That was the last time I ever saw Sully…

A Fellow Employee Connection!.................................

In November of that same year, with the passenger trains starting to come off, my job in the baggage room was abolished. I had to bump someone in the Division Superintendents Office, upstairs in the depot as the maintenance of way clerk, a very dull job. I wasn't happy about it, but It was the only job I could hold, and it did have Saturday and Sunday off, so that was a big plus.

I would start on my new job the Monday after Thanksgiving.

They nicknamed the office Stalag 17, because there was no talking unless it was railroad business, and most everyone walked around with a permanent frown on their face. Everyone that is except Virgil Wheeler, Mary Rose Carrig and me.

You had to work right up until 5:00pm. Not 4:59, but 5:00.

If you couldn't start another project, you still had to pretend like you were working on something, just the same. I was never good at faking work!

That Monday morning at 7:45, when I reported for my new job, the first person I saw was Marion Haas who was just another clerk in the office, but was someone who thought she ran the office.

In more ways than one, I guess, she did.

She was a tall, slender widow of about 62, with a pronounced limp and she could be quite brusque, until you got to know her, or more likely, until she got to know you, which took her some time.

She took one look at me and yelled out, "You're the one, you're that man!" "Look everyone, here he is, come over and see for yourself."

"You're the one who did it." Really! What have I done now, I wondered?

"We were all watching you all the time from right up here through the trackside windows."

"I don't have the slightest clue of what your talking about." "Just what exactly, have I supposedly done?" "No supposedly about it, you did it and we watched the whole thing, from right up here!"

"You're the man who rescued Bob Sullivan up off of ryans last Spring." "After he had fallen down drunk I suppose, and passed out."

"Then you put him in someone's car and took him home, I would guess." "Was Sully drunk?" "I can neither confirm nor deny that!" "You mean, you won't." "Yes, thats right! In any event, I mean I won't."

"Well anyway, we all watched the whole thing take place, from right up here." "We said at the time that whoever you were, you most likely were his Guardian Angel, who probably had just saved his life!"

"I don't think it was quite that bad, Mrs. Haas, and besides that was over seven months ago!" "I don't care how long ago it was, you saved his life and that's all there is to it, so please don't give me any more arguments about it!" "We were all just so thankful, that no freight for the yard had come along while he was lying over the tracks, such as he was." "At least not before you got him up and off that devilish track anyways." Whew, I thought. No sense saying anything more. She has won this argument hands down.

With that I asked her politely which desk was mine and reported for work. Yesem, Marion Haas was Ms. Daisy long before there even was a Ms. Daisy.

A Downstairs/Upstairs Depot Connection Had Now happened!.....

More Connections coming; When we lived on Collier St. for nearly two years during 1969 and 1970, our back yard backed up to Marion's backyard since she lived right around the corner, next to Guy and Ruth Stewart on Genesee St. Much more about Guy and Ruth in a later chapter.

In good weather, on the weekend Marion and I would talk with each other across the fence and I helped her fix some thing's in her back yard a couple of times. Bob Sullivan's name was never mentioned much, other than for her to tell me she knew Sully ever since she was a young girl. However, she did ask me one more time if Sully was drunk that day on ryans.

"Now Marion, I think weve been over this ground before." Seeing I was not going to tell her one way or the other, she dropped the subject all together.

Now a Co-Worker/Neighbor Connection!.............

Finally a third trick yard clerk position opened up in the westbound yard in the summer of 1969 and with my seniority I was able to hold it.

Finally after nineteen months, I was back around the trains I loved! Alleluia!!

SHORTY AT THE STATION

Belden Pratt was a short person, standing only about 5'2" tall. He had one hip or leg, that was shorter than the other, from birth that produced a noticeable limp. He was eighteen years older then me so he was forty-five at the time of this incident, while I was twenty-seven! Because of his short stature, almost everyone called him Shorty. At the time, he had a relief job that covered my job on my two days off which were Tuesday and Wednesday. His last responsibility for the day was working the baggage on Train #10 that ran from Buffalo, N.Y. to Hoboken, N.J.

Emmet Flansberg or Charlie as we called him was the night ticket agent. He would assist either me or Belden, in handling the baggage.

Believe me, a lot of these bags were quite heavy, some weighing up to 90lbs. Catalogs were printed in Hornell and then shipped all over the East.

Those bags were exceptionally heavy and quite bulky to boot!

Train #10 was due in the station at 6:40pm and out at 7:00pm.

On this hot and muggy, summer evening in 1967, I had taken Jean out to The Sunset Inn on East Avenue for dinner. I always picked my check up on Thursday mornings, when I came in to work. For some unknown reason I decided to stop by the depot, and pick it up, on this Wednesday evening, if they were in. Being out for the evening, I was dressed in a nice short sleeve shirt and dress pants.

About the time I showed up at the depot, Train #10 had just arrived from Buffalo. Charlie and Belden were just starting to work the baggage car.

I would have to wait until the train was gone to get my check, if they were even in.

While working passenger trains, the ticket office had to be locked up for security reasons. Quite understandable.

I stepped out on the trackside platform to see how things were progressing.

Belden was up on a fully loaded baggage wagon, throwing heavy sacks of mail, some loaded with catalogs into the west end of the baggage car.

Charlie was up on another wagon at the east end of the same baggage car.

I took one look at Belden and could see his face was all ashen grey.

I yelled up to him, "Belden, are you ok?" "Not really, Pete." "What's the matter Bel?" "I'm real short of breath and I have a slight pain in my chest that keeps coming and going."

"Climb down off that wagon Shorty and give me your gloves!"

"You can't be of any help here Pete, your not even on duty and besides that, you're all dressed up."

"It doesn't matter Belden." "No one knows I'm not on duty and we're certainly not going to tell them either!" "Come down from there right now, and don't worry about my clothes, they'll wash!" "What if the Trainmaster shows up Pete?" "Don't worry about that either Shorty, we'll cross that bridge when we come to it!"

Belden was right of course. I could be in some hot water if the Trainmaster showed up, with me doing the work while not being on duty! Sometimes though, living on the edge is fun!

At this moment in time though, Belden's physical condition, was much more paramount to me!

Taking his gloves and climbing up on the wagon, I advised him to go into the waiting room, get a cool drink of water, and just try to rest and relax a little and not worry about a thing. Charlie, looked over at me and gave me a big wink. He knew just exactly what I was trying to do! When I came back to work the next day, he told me he too was worried about Belden's physical condition until I showed up and took over!

It was so gosh darn hot and muggy, that in no time at all, sweat was running down my face, neck, chest and back!

Besides this not being an easy job, it was not a very clean one either.

In no time at all, my shirt and pants were getting sweaty and dirty too.

As I told Belden, I had no problem with that!

About the time we were done with the all work and #10 was finally on the move east once more, Jean was honking the horn, wondering what had happened to me since I was taking so long. I couldn't really blame her since I was probably gone for over twenty minutes, when I should have been gone for maybe two or three minutes, at the most!

When I finally got my check and got back to the car her first words to me were, "You're a mess, all sweaty and dirty. Have you been wrestling with someone or what?" " Well, yeah, I've been wrestling ok, but with ninety pound sacks of bulky catalogs and mail."

"How could you possibly get involved with that job tonight since your not even on duty right now?"

"It's a long story, I'll tell you all about it on the way home." "First, I've got to go and check on Belden Pratt in the waiting room."

I met Belden coming out of the waiting room door, feeling much better with color starting to come back into his face, and the pain in his chest all but gone.He said his breathing seemed a lot better too. "Are you sure your ok Shorty?" "Yeah thanks to you Pete, I am." "I'm just so glad that you decided to come by here tonight Pete!" "Me too Belden, me too."

"By the way Pete, why did you come by here tonight?" "I've never seen you on a Wednesday night before!" "Thats a good question Shorty".

Maybe Belden I came by here tonight just to help you out!" "But how did you know?" "Yeah, right Shorty, how did I know?" "Thats another good question, ONE that I don't have a quick answer for." "My guess, would be that karma brought me here!" "What's karma Pete?" "KARMA is fate or destiney Belden!" "You needed help, so I came!"

Another Fellow Employee Connection...........

Belden Pratt would die of a heart attack thirty years later in 1997 at the age of 75.

A Neighbor Down
and Under

Guy Stewart and his wife Ruth were great friends of my Grandmother Baker. In fact Grandma swore she was somehow related to Guy, or so she thought anyways. He was a Chief Train Dispatcher, employed by the Erie Railroad for many years. His office was located on the second floor of the depot. According to Grandma, he was the man who was going to pull some strings and hire me as a tower man for the railroad when I graduated from high school. It was gonna be signed, sealed and delivered.

Unfortunately for me, he retired in 1957 and I didn't graduate until 1958. So there was really nothing Guy could do now, since he was just another retiree instead of a very well respected Supervisor of Train Operations.

She had told me that somebody was going to help me get the railroad job in the tower, but she never told me who the man was until many years later.

In fact, it was a few years after Guy had passed away and his name came up in a conversation between her and I concerning him!

So at the time, I only knew Guy as just a nice, next door neighbor of ours for eighteen months. Someone who I conversed with many times, about railroading, politics, baseball, etc. He always offered me a drink of whiskey. "No thank you guy, not now, not ever!" was always my same reply!

I have to forward this story now to the Summer of 1970. We were living in a duplex on Collier St., next door to Ann Leary who owned the duplex. She was a widow and worked at the depot as a telephone operator for the Erie Lackawanna RR. Guy and Ruth lived on the corner of Collier and Genesee St, right next door to Marion Haas, (remember her?) who lived around the corner on Genesee St.

On the other side of us lived Bob Bishop, who you might also remember.

He was the midnight westbound yardmaster during that terrible blizzard back in February of 1961. Next door to Bob lived Bob and Doris Green. Bob was a railroad clerk at the storehouse. I was now hemmed in and Connected by railroad people living on all sides of me.

By now Guy and Ruth were quite elderly, but they still liked their martinis and cocktails. Sometimes I might add, a little bit too much for their own good.

One night in late July, I went to bed right after dinner since I was going to have to go to work at 11:00pm as the yardmaster in the westbound and then double through as a crew dispatcher from 7:00 to 3:00 the next day.

It would be a long sixteen hours of work for me, especially in this stifling heat, with no air conditioning available at work.

It was a hot, muggy evening and since we also had no air conditioning the windows were wide open with screens, hoping to catch a breeze, any breeze. Jean had taken the car and the kids down to her mother's for the evening, and wouldn't be home until it was time for me to go to work sometime around 10:30pm.

Around 8:30pm I was awakend by the squealing noise of brakes, plus a whole lot of screaming and yelling going on in the street just below my window.

The gist of the story was this; The Stewart's were out of whiskey and were going to the liquor store for more, with Ruth driving.

It seems that Guy had forgotten his wallet and told her to put the car in park and wait, while he went back in the house to retrieve it.

While he was getting out of the car, she accidentally put the car in reverse instead of park. The open passenger door jumped back, hitting Guy, and knocking him to the pavement. He was then somehow rolled under the car.

I'm not quite sure just how that happened, but he was definitely under the car now!

Ruth had her foot on the brake pedal now, but she didn't know exactly where Guy was, except she thought he was somewhere under the car, which he was. "What's going on down there," I yelled. "Pete, I just accidently knocked Guy down and backed over him."

"I think he's under the car somewhere!"

"Please, Pete, can you come here right now and help us?" "Don't move the car Ruth or take your foot off of the brake either, I'll be right down."

Quickly Putting on some clothes, I was down there in a flash.

When I got there, Ruth was quite hysterical and I could hear Guy moaning from somewhere under the car. I first made sure the gear shift was now in park, put the parking brake on and turned the ignition off. I then got Ruth out of the car and onto her side porch,while at the same time, giving her assurance, that everything was going to be ok.

Guy was now moaning and groaning, saying "I'm gonna die Pete, I just know I'm going to die." Looking under the car, I tried to also reassure Guy. "Your not going to die Guy, your going to be alright, just try and hang in there."

The only way to get him out was to crawl in after him. It wasn't going to be an easy job, but under the cricumstances, it was the only one that was now available!

Two things I found hard to believe about this scenario; How Guy ended up where he did and also the fact that he had not been run over by a wheel.

Both things were quite unreal, but the latter was very fortunate for Guy, my thoughts.

He was fully under the car, right in the middle of the frame, but as far as I could tell, no tire had passed over him!

"Don't worry Guy, I'm coming to get you out of there right now!"

Little by little I edged my way under the car face first to get him! Not an easy job, even though Guy and I were both pretty thin people.

When I finally got close to him, he blurted out "I'm so glad to see you Pete." "I'm glad to see you too Guy, but not under such circumstances!"

"Just how do you figure to get me out from under here Pete?" "Very carefully Guy, You'll see!" I advised him, when I move, to slide with me.

Little by little I edged our way out from under the car, holding onto his belt with my right hand, making sure to keep my left hand under the back of his head all the while, so his head didn't scrape the pavement. Finally, after what seemed like an eternity, we were both finally out from underneath the car!

It probably took only eight to ten minutes, but it seemed like forever to me!

I helped Guy up and over to his porch steps and sat him down.

He had a bloody nose and a couple of scrapes that I could see plus a lump on the back of his head. Even in this heat, Guy was shivering and I feared he was now going into shock. I had Ruth grab an afghan off their sofa and we wrapped it all around him, which helped him quite a bit.

By now, Ruth had gotten a grip on herself and tried to call Dr. Ethan Welch, who lived a short block away on the corner of Collier and Main St.

His line was continually busy so I sprinted down and told Doc what had happened and he said he would be right up.

When I got back, I reassured Guy that Dr. Welsh was on his way and he was going to be ok! Doc was there shortly with his little black doctors bag. The two of us helped Guy onto his sofa where Doc examined him thoroughly.

Outside of a bloody nose, a few bumps and abrasions, Doctor Welch pronounced Guy pretty much ok.

Ruth spokeup, "Well Guy it looks like no more drinks for us tonight."

"But I need one more tonight Ruth, especially after what's happened to me." Ruth told Guy she was too upset to drive anymore tonight.

"Look I don't have my car right now, but give me some money and your car keys and I'll go and get you something to drink." She went into the bedroom and came out with a twenty dollar bill. "We go to the liquor store right across from the depot." "Get us a bottle of scotch, it doesn't really matter what kind, except nothing cheap."

When I got back, Ruth met me at the door and told me Guy had gone to bed for the night. She thanked me for everything and said "I don't know what we would have done tonight, if not for you Pete." "You probably saved Guy's life."

"If not for your quick thinking, I probably would have accidently backed right on over him."

"That's all right Ruth, I'm just glad I was around and nothing worse happened." Both of them were now going to bed, but I was up for the night! There was absolutely no way I could have gotten back to sleep this night.

Not after all this excitement!

The next afternoon, Guy seemed as chipper as ever. He was waiting for me on his side porch, when I got home from work.

The first words out of his mouth were; "Would you like a drink of whiskey Pete?" "No thank you Guy." "Not now, not ever!"

He walked over and gave me a big hug as soon as he saw me and thanked me once again for all my help, from the night before. He told me he thought he was done for until I showed up. He reiterated once again that I had probably saved his life!

I don't know about that, but a sweet compliment it was anyways!

I was just glad everything had worked out for the good!
Another Neighbor Connection ....

I never knew that Guy was THE MAN, who was going to help me get the job in one of the towers on the railroad back in 1957, until sometime after he passed away many years later. Grandma Baker, for some unknown reason never told me who the man was until Guy's name came up in a conversation, we were having one day. She came out of left field at me with this one!

What an incredible Connection this story turned out to be!

Here was THE MAN who was going to help me get a railroad job in 1958, but couldn't because he retired the year before in 1957.

I ended up being the person thirteen years later in 1970 who quite possibly had saved his life. WOW, I thought. Just too unbelievable!

I never knew it at the time and neither did Guy, but I'm sure he does now!

What goes around, does come back around again, I guess, even if its thirteen years later! Also remember there was a total thirteen year (1961 to 1974) gap in saving the six lives! I guess thirteen should be my lucky number!

Another Unbelievable Connection to say the Least!....

You can't make this stuff up!!

A Gap of Thirteen Years, Finally Connected!................

I've played this scene over in my mind many times and I think I've come up with the reason Guy ended up under his car in the first place.When he was knocked to the pavement, he was half under the car and half out. Thinking Ruth was going to back up, he scooted the best he could, under the car towards the middle so no wheel would pass over his body.

This seemed like a good move on his part to me!

FROM LOCKPORT
TO LEWISBURG

I was already a board certified junior varsity basketball official starting out in the basketball season of 1963-64. To become a certified varsity official, which enabled you to work high school varsity games along with college and professional games, you had to first score a floor test of 90 or better and then pass a written test of fifty true or false questions. You could only miss six out of the fifty questions. There are only ten basic rules in the game of basketball, but out of those ten rules can come close to 300,000 different game situations.

I had no problem passing the floor test, scoring 94 the first year, 98 the second year and another 98, this third year. The written test was another hard challange entirely. The test was tough and it was meant to be tough.

The test cost $20.00 to take and the fee was non-refundable if you failed it.

It was given only once a year on the first Monday in December.

If you failed it, you had to wait for another full year to come around, to be able to take it again. The first year, (1968) I missed seven questions, or one too many. The second year (1969) I missed it by eight. I was very disappointed, because I had studied for so long and so hard and now it seemed that I was regressing. Very disappointing, to say the least.

The test in our county was always given at 7:00pm at Bath, N.Y., the County Seat. I decided to leave home at 5:30pm, drive over to Molly's Diner on the western outskirts of Bath, have a coffee or two, and brush up a bit on the rule book. I also wanted to try and gather my thoughts. Just try to relax a little too, if that was at all possible. Leaving Hornell, I turned onto the Big Creek Road, that would take me to Bath on this dark and cold first Monday in December of 1970.

After making the turn, I noticed two young boys, about fifteen or sixteen, along the shoulder of the road attempting to hitch a ride. What on God's green earth are these two kids doing out here in the cold, at this time of night? I pulled over and they ran up and opened the front passenger side door. "Can you give us a lift mister?"

"It all depends, where are you guys going?" Lewisburg, Pa."

"Where are you coming from?" "Lockport, N.Y. do you know where that is?"

Without any further hesitation, on my part, "Get in the car!"

"I hope you both realize this isn't the best weather or time of day to be out here doing this."

The older boy took over the conversation. "It doesn't matter we just had to do it." It seems the one boys mother was married to the other boys father and neither one of them could get along at all with their step parent. "What are you going to Lewisburg for?" The older boy spoke up once again.

"My father is a prison guard at the Pennsylvania State Penitentiary there and we are going down to live with him and my stepmother."

"Really, does your father know that your coming?" "Nope!" "Well, I want to wish you guys a lot of luck on that one."

The younger boy of the two pulled out a baby ruth candy bar and asked the older lad, if they could split it up between them now, because he was pretty hungry.

The older boy told him to put it away until they were really desperate.

"Have you guys had anythingto eat at all today?" "We've been on the road since 9:30 this morning mister and we each had an apple and a candy bar sometime around 12:30."

"Do you have any money between the two of you?" "Nope."

I then proceded taking them to Molly's Diner and bought them both an order of a cheeseburger, french fries and a milk shake, along with two candy bars and a banana and apple each, to take with them. We had a long talk and I told them they should try to see things from their step parents perspective point of view. I advised them to try and get along somehow, and try to work things out with the parents. They told me they would think it over and take my advice under consideration!

When they were finished, I took them to the eastern outskirts of Bath and wished them good luck and cautioned them to be careful. I then rushed to the Bath Central School, getting there at 6:58, just in time to take my test.

I don't know what ever happened to those two kids, but over the years, I wondered about them a lot from time to time and hoped and prayed that things worked out ok for them!

Just so no good deed is always punished, I passed the test this time with flying colors, missing just one question. With the kids, I had no time to relax or any time at all to brush up on some things that might be on the test.

Hard to figure out. I think someone was pulling hard for me to pass this test. Maybe someone with wings!

Just for the record, my old girlfriend was now married and living where? You guessed it, Lockport, N.Y. Connected Yet Again From Afar!....................

This time by a couple of kids who were complete strangers to me, and who in all probability, I would never see again.

Just so no good deed never goes unpunished, when I got home that night and told Jean the story about the kids, she gave me a big dressing down for picking the boys up in the first place. "They

could have stabbed you or worse yet, shot you and stole the car."
"You should never have picked them up to begin with." Yeah right,
my thoughts.

Maybe today I wouldn't pick anyone up, but back then things
were somewhat different. In fact, a whole lot different.

Besides they looked like pretty good kids to me!

An Air Traffic Controller Grounded

I was driving the railroad jitney, as the clerk/messenger, one day in May of 1974. As I was leaving the westbound yard parking lot, I happened to notice a man exiting from my good friend John Todd's parked, unlocked car.

He appeared to put something under his jacket, but from the distance, I couldn't tell exactly what it was. John, who you remember from the Sunday School Basketball League (SSBL) was at his job as a car inspector for the railroad in the car repair yard. This facility was located at the west end of the eastbound yard. This location was just about where I had parked my car, during the big blizzard of 1961.

He had parked his unlocked car in the westbound parking lot instead of the eastbound as was his usual place. I suppose he did this so he could purchase some cigarettes at the railroad bunkhouse, located on the hill just behind the westbound yard office. John was the epitome of a chain smoker, if there ever was one. Much of the time he would light one cigerette off of the other.

Sad to say but the cigerettes would be part responsible for his demise.

I was on my way up to the diesel shop to pick up an inbound engine crew, and bring them back to the yard parking lot for their cars.

I stopped and motioned for the stranger to come over to the jitney.

"Please get in, I would like to talk to you." He got in and asked me if I was the railroad dick, which was the slang word for a railroad policeman.

"No I am not."

"What do you have under your jacket?" "Nothing!" "Look, I saw you come out of that car over there and put something under your jacket, so you might just as well come clean right here and now about it!"

"I'm sorry, I didn't mean to do it." With that confession, he pulled out a pair of men's dress shoes, he had taken from John's car.

"I didn't mean to take them, but I'm a little bit down on my luck!"

"Where are you coming from anyways?" "I came in on a westbound freight from New York, (City) and I'm trying to get back to Detroit through Buffalo."

He didn't look like a bum to me, at least any typical bum that I had seen in the past, hanging around the railroad, from time to time.

He was about forty five years old with a full head of red hair, stood about 5'6 and weighed around 140lbs. Of most importance to me, he had a kind face!

I was driving and doing some deep thinking while he was doing most of the talking.

His story was; He was a former Air Traffic Controller from Detroit who had lost his job due to heavy drinking, brought on by stress on the job.

In the process, he had lost his house. His wife had divorced him and took off with their two kids, a boy and a girl for parts unknown.

He was now trying to get back home, to get some much needed therapy and see if he could somehow patch things up with the wife.

Maybe in the process, he could get another chance with his job too, or so he hoped! Not a very nice story to learn about, were my thoughts.

"Are you going to turn me in to the railroad or the city police?" "Nope, I'm not going to turn you in to anyone." "Have you had anything at all to eat recently?" "No, I don't have any money!" "I was going to try and sell these shoes to get some money to eat with." "Where are you taking me anyways?"

"Do you like hot dogs?" "Sure, who doesn't!" "We have some of the best hot dogs in the world up town at the Texas Hots Restaurant."

I then proceeded to drive up to The Texas and got him two dogs to go with the works, (onions and sauce) plus an extra large coffee and took him to the far reaches of North Hornell, by the Big Creek Road.

I could now be in some trouble myself on two counts.

Number one, this fellow wasn't a railroad employee and therefore, he shouldn't have even been in the vehicle, because of insurance reasons!

Secondly, Hornell not North Hornell, was the furthest limits I could drive the jitney, unless so authorized to do so. I was wrong on that count too!

However If any rules were ever meant to be bent just a little, these were certainly the ones, were my thoughts!

After he finished eating, I gave him ten bucks, wished him good luck in all his future endeavors and told him to try and bum a car ride to Buffalo and then on to Detroit, if at all possible.

I also cautioned him about hanging around rail yards, which at times, could be quite dangerous places to be. One mistake or slip and you could lose an arm, leg or WORSE, your life!

Quite surreal was the fact that I let this soul OUT of the jitney at the very same spot where I had picked UP the two hitch-hiking teenagers from Lockport a few years back. One Special Connection, Trumped by yet Another Special Connection!........

You can't make this stuff up!

When leaving the jitney, he thanked me from the bottom of his heart and left me with this parting statement; "Why aren't there more good and caring people like you in the world?"

I gave him a thumbs up and drove off, with tears welled up in my eyes!

I said a silent prayer that things would work out for him back in Detroit.

After picking up the engine crew at the diesel shops and depositing them at the westbound parking lot, I drove over to the eastbound cripple yard.

I handed my friend John his dress shoes, advising him he had better keep his car locked up from now on. John stood there smoking a cigarette, as was his usual thing to do, just as unconcerned as a lark.

He told me, he would take my suggestion, under serious advisement.

Yeah right, so much for that, my thoughts!

Two people I had helped and Connected with in one day.

Both for far different reasons! One person who I thought the world of and one person who I had never seen before and who I would never see again!

Two Good Connections For The Price of One!..............

John and Helen Todd had five sons. Their second oldest son Douglas was born the same year as me, 1940.

While John was far away on a ship in the Pacific in 1944, during World War Two, little four year old Dougie ran out in the road chasing a ball and was struck and killed by a U.S. Postal truck. I always thought John took me under his wing because I reminded him of the son he lost, same age and all.

Funny thing; John and I agreed on hardly anything. He was Republican, I was Democrat. He was anti this and anti that (or so he said) while I was anti nothing.

He was a heavy smoker, I never smoked at all.

Sometimes I think he just liked to make a lot of noise or try to get my goat.

He was quite good at both of these things too!

But in spite of all this different stuff, the true fact of the matter was, we thought the world of each other!

He lived less then a mile from the yard office. If he couldn't sleep, he would get up at anytime of the night, and come down to the bunkhouse.

After buying a pack of cigarettes and two cups of coffee (One for each of us) he would come in the yard office and bend my ear for an hour or more.

At 3:00am or whenever, It didn't really matter. Just too funny for words.

Everyone came to the bunkhouse or the westbound yard office!

Why? Because they were always open 24/7/365!

By the way, John and I did agree on one thing. We both took cream and sugar in our coffee! Hurray for that!

My good friend John, would pass away at age 64 on May 20th, from mesothelioma, a form of cancer, that is caused by asbestos. He had served on a ship in the Navy, in the Pacific theatre, during the War. Maybe that's where he contacted his terrible disease.

I would be a pall barer at his funeral on May 23rd, 1977 my 37th birthday.

Needless to say, It was one pretty sad birthday for me!

Another Connection, This Time Not a Good One.........................

Now 37 years later I'm writing this book!

37 points was the single game record when I was one point short in 1958!

You can't make this stuff up!

TWO KIDS AND A TRUCK

In the summer of 1974, we were living at 111 Maple St., a home which we purchased in September of 1970. Two small toddlers age three and two lived two doors up from us with their mother and father. There was a house in between us at that was inhabited by six elderly sisters. Three of the ladies were widows, while the other three had never married.

They had a short sidewalk of about forty feet.

I tried to keep their sidewalk shoveled off for them in the Winter, which they greatly appreciated. It just so happened that their father had been an engineer on the Erie Railroad out of Binghamton, N.Y. They told me of his many exploits, when they were young girls.

A Nice Neighborly Connection here................

This summer day, I was on my way up town to pay some bills and run some other errands. As I was coming out of my front door, I happened to glance up just in time to see the two kids come tearing out of their front door, down their steps and head for the road.

The cars in front of their house were parked elephant style or one right after the other. In this way, if someone walked or ran between the parked cars out into the street, a vehicle coming down the road, would not be able to see them until it was way to late to avoid hitting them.

Coming down the road this day, was a large garbage truck.

I dropped everything I had in my hands on the porch, jumped my railing and sprinted toward the kids who were about to run out between two of the parked cars, and into the road. Because they were so little, they never realized, that there was a truck, that was bearing right down on them.

It was the perfect storm for one tragic accident!

I had but one chance. I had better not muff it, my thoughts. As I came to a skidding stop, I had to be careful that my momentum did not push them along with me into the path of the oncoming truck. I reached out and grabbed the two of them by the back of the nap of their tee shirt, one in each hand and fell back, the three of us in a heap, out of harms way just as the truck slammed on its brakes and slid on past us by about ten feet.

The driver jumped out of the truck and ran between two of the parked cars towards me. His face was pure white with fear. "Did I hit those two kids?" "No but it was mighty close." "I couldn't really see them until the last second." "I know, they couldn't see you either." The truck driver told me it would take him a few minutes to gather his bearings, before he could drive away. "I understand how you feel, take your time," was my reply.

The mother, hearing the squeal of the brakes, along with all the ruckus, came running out of her front door asking "What's all the noise and commotion about?" "These kids almost got hit by this garbage truck, that's what just happened." "I was upstairs making the beds and the last thing I knew they were right there with me." "These kids are very active. I think I would consider locking the front door from now on unless they're right next to you." "If I hadn't been coming out of my house at the same time, this would have been one terrible tragedy!"

A Neighborly Connection Once Again.................

When we left Hornell in June of 1981 for Allentown, Pa., where I had been transferred with the railroad, five of the six sisters who lived next door to us in 1970, had by then passed away.

Another Sad Connection Here!.................

THE UP-TOWN GRILL

You say you don't believe that things happen for a reason!

Wait until you check this one out! This situation definitely happened for a reason, and a very special reason it turned out to be!

While living in Utica, N.Y. for a little over four years, we had a fish fry (haddock) dinner almost every Friday night at the Up-Town grill, just off of Genesee St. It was a very unique place to say the least. There were booths on both side's of the restaurant, a few tables down the middle and a two chair table right next to the door that was forever opening and closing with people coming and going!.

This table location was definitely not the place to be if the weather was foul!

Upon your arrival, you had to go to the back and sign your name on a clipboard hanging there, along with any seat preference you might have.

It was on a first come, first serve basis. After signing in you had to wait for a seat by standing in the isle right next to the people that were already seated and/or were eating. Not a good setup to be sure, but the food was excellent and the price was reasonable so it was well worth any wait or discomfort one might suffer.

We would usually arrive there sometime around 6:00pm, sign in and wait our turn, sometimes long, sometimes short!

There were six ladies who also came every Friday night too. The oldest lady rode with her single mom daughter, who was a bank executive. The other four ladies were either related to the older lady or were her friends. They told us they got there early, sometime around 4:30 to 5:00pm, every Friday.

Their reason for doing this was two-fold; They wanted to be sure of a booth, without any wait and they also wanted to get a head start on their cocktails, prior to dinner. We didn't know their names, and we were never formally introduced to them, but by striking up a conversation one night, it seemed like we had known them forever.

On this cold, rainy, late October evening I signed us up for a booth, even though we were a few times out for one.

The six ladies minus one, the bank executive, were seated in the front booth on the right side, next to the two chair table, but out of the grasp of the cold wind. One of the waitresses poked me in the back and said, "Pete, we can get you the table up by the door right now." "You sit there often anyways."

"No thanks honey, the weather is just too nasty to sit by that door tonight."

After an hour wait I noticed people being seated in booths, that had come in and had signed up after us! I went on back to the clipboard to see if we had been bypassed or what. What I found out was dumbfounding!

We had been passed over by five other couples whose names had been crossed out below ours! I asked two waitress' what happened and they swore they both never saw our name there, but now they did. One said we could have the next booth that became vacant, regardless!

The little table by the door was still open. No one was using it on this cold and blustery night. I told her we would take it even though we didn't much care for it, because frankly, by now, we were a little tired of waiting, and also a little hungry too.

As we sat down, we said our hello to the five ladies. We made some small talk with them, while waiting for our dinner to come. Every time that door opened or shut, I cringed because of the foul weather it let in and I was directly in its path. Sitting to my right, Jean was out of most of the wind.

About the time we were finishing up dinner, four of the ladies, were now waiting for one of their husbands to come and pick the four of them up.

The older lady was waiting for her bank executive daughter to come for her.

Presently, the matriarch got a phone call from her daughter.

The daughter couldn't get away from this important meeting for another hour or two, to come and pick her up. She also had a much more pressing problem. She needed her mom to call a taxi and go and get her seventeen year old son who was sick with a high fever of 103 degrees and take him to the St. Elizabeth Hospital ER. By this time the ride for the other four ladies had come and they were gone.

When she came back to her seat in a now empty booth, she was beside herself. She had called for a taxi and was told, on account of the bad weather, she would have a one to two hour wait at the earliest, maybe even longer.

"Look, we've finished eating. We'll take you to pick up your grandson and take the two of you to the ER." "Oh I don't want to put you people out." " Trust me, youre not putting us out one bit."

With that, the three of us left and went to pick up the grandson.

We then proceeded to take him to the ER. I went in with them. I told the grandmother we would wait for them if need be, it was not a problem.

She called her daughter to let her know they were at the ER, and the daughter told her she would be able to meet them at the ER within the hour, so it wasn't necessary for us to wait around any longer.

She wanted to pay me the taxi fare rate, but of course I told her no way that was going to happen!

"Here's our phone number." "Please call us up in the morning and let us know how you made out with your grandson."

The next morning the grandmother called us up thanking us so much for what she called an act of mercy, the night before.

She said her grandson had a bad upper respiratory infection and was put on antibiotics. His fever had now gone down to 99, and he was feeling somewhat better.

Stop and think for a minute how this divine intersession happened, along with everything that had to fall into line for it to take place!

If we HADN'T been passed over five times for a booth, we would have eaten our dinner and been long gone from the restaurant. If we HAD taken the small table by the door at the earliest time offered us instead of the latest, once again we would have eaten and been gone!

If we hadn't taken the small table by the door an hour later, we wouldn't have known anything about the grandmothers plight.

If I hadn't survived in 1960, none of it would have mattered here in 1986, anyways for none of it would have taken place. She might have been left waiting for a taxi or the daughter to come for her unless someone else stepped up to the plate to help her.

In this special scenario, my being in the right spot at the right time, once again, was a good place for a grandmother and her grandson, who was in need of medical attention!

Another Meant To Be Connection!..

Once again, no way to make this stuff up!

An Operation Up In Smoke!

Don Virginia was a Conrail railroad conductor out of Syracuse, N.Y. He was a real nice guy to work with. He was also quite a heavy smoker and every time I talked with him over the phone, it always sounded like he was smoking, which he was. He was about my age and with his seniority, Don was able to hold what was called, an interdivisional run from Selkirk, (Albany) N.Y. to Buffalo ,N.Y. and return the next day.

One of the hardest parts of this job was the fact he had to drive about 150 miles to start his run at Selkirk, and of course the same distance back home, at the end of his round trip.

I would try to alert him approximately when he was about to be called for work so he could start out a little early to make it to Selkirk on time, since the drive alone was a little over two hours! The official call time itself was usually only two hours. He fully appreciated what I did to look out for him! Especially with the bad weather in upstate New York in the Winter time!

I can't remember which year, but one day in either 1994 or 1995, he called me up to mark off due to the fact he was going into the hospital for vascular surgery on his legs in two days. He had a circulation problem in both legs and they were going to clean the veins out with surgery. He told me he would keep in touch and call me in about three weeks after the surgery. I wished him well and told him I would say a little prayer that everything would work out just fine for him!

Don called me up one morning about three weeks later with some munch different information concerning his health. It ended up he had some blockage in the arteries to his heart that had to be taken care of first and he was now waiting for another three weeks to have the legs attended to. "Don, you're still smoking, aren't you?" "Yeah, but how can you tell?" "Hey Don, I talk to a couple of hundred men every day and I can easily tell the smokers from the non-smokers!"

"Don, I had a good friend that worked with me here in this office, Paul Inman, age 59 and he had the same operation that your going to have. He had had one heart attack previously. He was a heavy smoker, just like you." "I don't mean to scare you, but he had a heart attack and died right on the operating table!" "In your case, I think it would be a good idea for you to stop smoking at least for the time being if not for good!" "Especially after all the trouble you've been having" "But of course, that's entirely up to you!"

Three plus weeks later Don was in the hospital on a Sunday evening, waiting to have surgery on his legs early the next morning. That night at 8:30pm, a nurse-anesthesiologist was there explaining to him, the anesthesia he was going to use for Don's operation the next morning. Before leaving, he asked Don if he could check the pulse rate on his feet. Don said sure, go ahead! After feeling the pulse in both feet twice at 72, which was perfect circulation, he stated to Don that he felt he no longer needed the second operation!

To be positive though, he went and called the surgeon at home and had him come over to the hospital to check the matter out! The surgeon not being home, the nurse left word on his answering machine.

The Surgeon, when he finally showed up at 10:30pm concurred with the nurse's opinion and asked him if he had done anything different in the interim since the first operation on his heart to the present? Don told the doctor, the only thing he could think of that he had done different, was he had quit smoking, cold turkey!

"But you told me you couldn't quit smoking!" "What made you change your mind?" "A good friend of mine on the railroad told me a story that scared the bejeebers out of me and besides that I greatly respected his opinion! So I am trying to quit." "And so far so good Doc!"

Well you can tell your friend, he just saved you from a second operation!" "You can get up, get dressed and go home." "Doc, my girlfriend went to bed at 8:30pm tonight because she was going to be here in the morning at 6:00am for my operation." "I hate to wake her up this late, have her get dressed and come and get me." "Would it be ok if I stayed here tonight and went home in the morning instead?" "Sure Don, that's fine!" "Besides, they've already charged your insurance for the room tonight anyways!"

The next morning around 9:00am, Don all excited, called me up at work. I noticed right away, that he wasn't smoking, which I thought was a good sign. "Pete, I want you to know that I don't have to have that second operation now and you're the main reason for it." "You saved me from having the operation on my legs for the circulation problem I was having."

"How do you figure I did that Don?" "Well you scared me so much with that story of your late friend, coupled with your concern for me, that right after I hung up with you, I decided to quit smoking cold turkey. And so far it seems to be working." "It wasn't me Don, it was you. " "After all Don, you're the one that quit smoking!"

"Yes that's very true Pete, but if I hadn't called you up that morning, three weeks ago and talked with you, I would never have quit and I would be under the anesthesia right about now!" "Thanks to you Pete, you saved me from undergoing surgery for a second time!"

"Hey Don, how does it sound, if we say that both of us, you and me together, saved you from a second operation!"

"I'll go for that Pete, but I still wouldn't have stopped smoking if I hadn't made that phone call to you three weeks ago"

Once again, if I hadn't survived, this CONNECTION would never have been made and Don would have been under the knife again!

So you might say, this latest operation went up in smoke!

You can't make this stuff up!

My Friend Charles

My friend Charles was born in the Panama Canal Zone in 1943. He was from a third generation of Americans who were born there. His grandfather helped build the original canal and his father also worked there for many years.

When he was in his late teens, he migrated to New Jersey to live with a grandparent. He and I became friends while working part time at a sporting goods store in Estero, Fl. Since Charles is nuts over anything connected with trains, I give him my three train magazines, I get every month, when I am finished with them. I work Monday through Thursday and Charles usually works Saturday and Sunday so we don't see much of each other. On Saturday, May 10, 2014 he was working a shift from 5:00pm to 10:00pm. Somehow he misplaced one of our scan guns we all use to scan prices, make sale signs, price merchandise, etc. These scan guns cost $2,500 apiece, which is a pretty expensive piece of equipment, especially if one gets lost.

When closing the store that evening at 10:00pm, he along with the other employees looked all over the store for the scanner, but couldn't find it. Needless to say, because of the cost of replacement, Charles would be in hot water if the gun was either lost or stolen.

I became aware of the lost scanner when I came to work the following Monday, May 12.Off and on all day, I looked all over the store for it, when I had the chance. I would say for about a total of forty-five minutes, with no luck. All during the following week, we all looked for the scanner, when we had the time, with a negative result and the managers feared the gun had now been stolen.

I for one didn't think so. I thought the gun would eventually surface, even though I had looked high and low for it, for days. When I left work on Thursday, May 15 at 5:00pm the gun was still missing.

The scan gun is black in color, so it blends in well with many of the products we sell. We wish they were orange or yellow or some other bright color. It would also be nice if it had a beeper, so we could call them, when one goes missing.

When I reported back to work on Monday, May19, the scanner was still absent. An assistant manager told me to forget looking for it, the gun was long gone and we were not going to find it, end of story!

The store had been turned upside down for over a week now, trying to locate it, to no avail.

I spent another twenty minutes on Monday looking for it, all for naught.

When I arrived for work the next day, Tuesday May20th, I asked the manager on duty, if the gun had been found yet.

The shake of his head indicated no to me.

He also reiterated his opinion, which was the scanner was gone, possibly stolen and in all probability, would never be found.

Too much time had gone by for it to surface!

After I clocked in and started out on the floor to my station in footwear, I said a very short prayer and added a small thought!. "Dear Lord, please do me a HUGE favor, and help US find the scan gun today, if only for Charles sake." "I just have a funny feeling that its here somewhere."

I wasn't out on the floor three minutes, looking for it on my way to my station in footwear, when to my complete surprise, I was drawn like a magnet to some red, fold up athletic stadium chairs. These are the kind that fold all up and fit in a sack, with a tie string at the end.

Pulling these chairs out and wide apart, lo and behold, there the scanner was, way in the back. It was somehow tucked in behind a bunch of these stadium fold up chairs. A few of our fellow workers, including our store manager said they had looked in this location before and found it hard to believe that was the place I found it.

If you just stuck your hand in between the chairs a little, you would have easily missed it.

The chairs had to be separated and spread apart to locate the scanner.

Just one more important thing in my time, I had to do and with Gods help, it got done! I didn't save anyone's life this time or even come close, but with a big assist from the Lord, I may have just saved Charles his job, while also alleviating a ton of worry from his mind in the process!

If I had perished in 1960 would the scanner ever have been found? Maybe so, maybe no! I think for sure in time, but who knows when?

Probably long after Charles had been let go!

An Associate/Friend/Lord Connection.............................

Our store manager told me aside, that I had indeed saved Charles his job, because the security guy for the company, who has the last word on something like this, wanted to fire him and would have if the scan gun had not been found!

EPILOGUE -
MAKE A DIFFERNCE

I'm sure, we all wonder, from time to time, whether our lives have made a difference of any kind, during our time on earth, however long or short our lives may be!

Especially when ones life is on the downward side of the mountain! Have we helped our fellow human beings out, to the best of our ability in every way, shape or manner, that we possibly could!

In my own lifetime, I know that I made a difference, a huge difference in a myriad of all kinds of ways to help many people out!

For starters, I helped raise four children into responsible and caring adults. From those four children have come six Grandchildren. The main keeper of these children, of course was their mother!

If I had perished back in 1960, none of these sweet people would be here today. This is one big difference in and of itself for me! Thanks be to God for that!

The five situations whereby I helped save six peoples lives would definitely stand out as proud accomplishments in my lifetime for sure!

There were also many other important things, that took place, in the years that followed my miraculous comeback from death's door.

All of those great and good things that happened with my involvement, only occured because I somehow was able, with the Lords help, to pull through the critical illness I suffered with!

But surely, wasn't that how it was all supposed to play out anyways!

Think about these important SET OF FACTS for just a moment.

If I was going to have a near death experience, (which I had) coupled with the all important thought conversation with the special Angel,(which I also had) then the ruptured appendix I suffered had to be part and parcel in the whole scheme of things!

Everything and everyone that was Connected with me was meant to happen, just the way it did! Call it karma, call it whatever you want. Whatever it was, it was prescribed in Heaven!

Even Dr. James Kelly falling back to sleep was part of the equation too!

Take one thread out of this woven material and the whole thing starts to unravel.

It was ALL meant to be just the way it went down! I know this for sure, because in my life and time, I lived the whole thing out!

Two months before my NDE actually took place, I talked a friend, into going with me and two other friends to a Girl Scout camp, where he met his future wife and mother of his children. If I hadn't persisted so hard and so long, he wouldn't have gone and they wouldn't have ever met, not in a million years.

Something made me keep trying to get him to change his mind, a whole lot longer than almost anyone, including myself, should have!

Someone or something much bigger then both of us, intervened here and made Bill Pearson change his mind into going!

Divine Intervention Was Hard At Work Here!................

Looking back In time, I know now just what the Angel meant when he laid this short but all powerful message on me: YOU MUST GO BACK PETER. ITS NOT YOUR TIME, AND YOU HAVE MANY IMPORTANT THINGS TO DO!

It is quite possible this Angel was ST. RAPHAEL, the Arch Angel who is in charge of all Angels!

Maybe the big boss took on this special job! Someone important sure did, because I certainly had a lot of help in all of those life saving endeavors!

Funny thing, but I never CONNECTED all the dots of my NDE, with my helping to save those six peoples lives until many years later, sometime in the late 1970's. To tell the truth, it never even crossed my mind about all those Connections that I had been involved with until then. Maybe because they were spread out over a thirteen year period!

Once again I tried opening up and telling people about my NDE plus all the CONNECTIONS that OCCURED with me afterwards.

Everything ended up just as the Angel had stated to me it would!

I had never given anything a second thought when it was all taking place.

To me, it was just doing what we're all supposed to do. Nothing more, nothing less. I believe the Lord chose me in helping to save those six peoples lives for the following reasons:

He knew I would PERSIST in finding Sue in that snowy field, once I fully realized she was really out there in that precarious location!

He knew my grit and determination would carry the day, during that brutal blizzard, even while at the same time, my incision was paining me something wicked! He knew with my tenacious spirit, there was no way, I would give up on her on that night!

He allowed me to easily hear her pleas above the storm, while no one else heard ANYTHING! I guess, this was the way it was all meant to be! No other way to put it!

He gave me the much needed STRENGTH, to pull Joe out of and away from his smoking car.

He knew I would disobey the direct command of my two superiors in order to RESCUE Sully up off that live railroad track.

189

He knew I would get involved, even after they ordered me not too!

He put me in the right room that summer evening to hear the Stewarts dilema down in the driveway right below me. The night, that Guy was knocked down by his car door, and then somehow rolled under the car!

He knew I was just little enough to fit under that car to pull Guy out.

He knew I had the speed and quickness to pluck those two toddlers out of harms way of the ONCOMING garbage truck.

He made sure I didn't muff the one and only chance I had to skid to a stop, grab them and fall back.

He knew Shorty needed help at the depot. Thats why he sent me!!

The Lord knew, because He knows ALL things and unlike us mortals,

HE never makes any mistakes.

When I was in the 6th grade at the Bryant Elementary School, I volunteered to be a patrol boy (crossing guard) for the other kids safety, while they were crossing the streets, near the school. I wanted the responsibility for what I thought was an important job.

An important job it was too!

Much to my disappointment I was never selected for this important duty.

I would guess, it was because of my small stature.

The Lord made up for this gaffe in later years, by giving me much more responsibility then I ever needed or maybe even wanted!

He sure presented me with a lot of hurdles to run over!

I would like to think, with His assistance along with the Angels timely help I cleared them all! In fact, when looking back on every thing that happened, I'm positive I did!

All of those situations that I was so CONNECTED with, happened a long time ago, but who knows, maybe just maybe, the Lord isn't finished with me yet. After all, the incident with my friend

Charles happened just this past May, two months AFTER I started writing this book.

Something recently happened on September 14th of 2014 that required my help, once again. A neighbor friend of ours had a stroke and is in the hospital! Her husband who is on a walker called me up and asked if we could help him out at this difficult time by walking their dog, a couple of times a day. Since NO was never in my vocabulary, you know the rest of the story, as Paul Harvey would say!

Always remember how much we are all Connected with each other.

Never forget what happens to all of us, good or bad, through these Connections! Its up to each of us, with the Lords help of course, to try and make sure, in one way or another these Connections,end up being GOOD CONNECTIONS!................